PUBLIC ADMINISTRATION AND POLICY ANALYSIS

Public Administration and Policy Analysis

Recent Developments in Britain and America

R. A. W. RHODES

University of Essex

Gower

First published by Saxon House, Teakfield Limited.

Reprinted 1981 by Gower Publishing Company Limited, Croft Road, Aldershot, Hants, GU11 3HR, England

British Library Cataloguing in Publication Data

Rhodes, R. A. W.
    Public administration and policy analysis.
    1. Public administration – Study and teaching –
    United States   2. College teaching – United
    States   3. Policy sciences – Study and teaching –
    United States   4. Public administration – Study
    and teaching – Great Britain   5. College teaching –
    Great Britain   6. Policy sciences – Study and
    teaching – Great Britain
    I. Title
    350'.0007'1173   JF1338.A2

    ISBN 0-566-00239-6

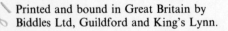
Printed and bound in Great Britain by
Biddles Ltd, Guildford and King's Lynn.

Contents

1 INTRODUCTION   1

2 THE SCOPE OF AMERICAN PUBLIC ADMINISTRATION
IN THE 1970s   6

     Introduction   6

     Organisational Humanism   10

     Political Theory in Public Administration   13

     The New Political Economy   16

     Conclusions   18

3 A ROSE BY ANY OTHER NAME: THE SEARCH FOR
POLICY ANALYSIS   23

     Introduction   23

     The Role of Social Scientists in Policy-making   28

     The Theories of Decision-making   30

     Conclusions   35

4 TEACHING PUBLIC ADMINISTRATION AND POLICY
ANALYSIS IN AMERICA   40

     Introduction   40

     The Institutional Backcloth   40

     The Individual Schools   43

     Conclusions   59

5 PUBLIC ADMINISTRATION AND POLICY ANALYSIS IN
BRITAIN   68

     Introduction   68

     'The Missing Tradition'   69

     The Scope of British Public Administration in
the 1970s   71

     Teaching Public Administration and Policy Analysis
in Britain   78

Conclusions   86

6 SOME LESSONS FROM AMERICA ?   94

APPENDICES

1 The Core Courses of the Masters' Programmes   104

2 Recent Masters' Degrees in Public Policy
   in British Universities   113

Author Index   116

Subject Index   119

1 Introduction

The last decade has been one of ferment in the study of Public
Administration   There have been many new developments in both Britain
and the United States of America.   This monograph surveys these
intellectual developments and, in particular, explores innovations in
teaching and curriculum design.

Between September and December 1975 I had the opportunity to visit
several American universities specialising in teaching public affairs,
public administration and public policy.   The masters' programmes at
the universities of Syracuse, Michigan, California (Berkeley) and
Stanford are the centre-piece of this study. (1)   I compare the
content of, and the teaching methods employed in, these various
programmes.   However, no teaching programme can be considered in
isolation from the intellectual climate within which it is taught.   In
the first instance, therefore, I provide a survey of intellectual
developments in American Public Administration.   I have not attempted
to document every development in detail.   The emphasis falls in
depicting the backcloth against which the various teaching innovations
took place.

The main development of the last decade is the emergence of policy
analysis; at times it seemed the only important development.   It
represents a direct challenge to existing departments of Public
Administration.   Even to suggest to members of American policy analysis
schools that they were studying Public Administration was to invite at
best a sermon and at worst invective on the ills and inadequacies of
Public Administration.   And yet a school of policy analysis and a
department of Public Administration could have virtually identical
teaching programmes.   In addition to describing policy analysis,
therefore, it is also necessary to pose the question of how it differs
from Public Administration.(2)

The discussion of the nature of policy analysis is of direct
relevance to all those concerned with the development of Public
Administration in Britain.   Recent years have seen a debate about the
creation of a 'British Brookings'.   This attempt to found a major
school of policy analysis in Britain limped its way through the pages of
the Times Higher Educational Supplement for some two years before it
foundered in the shallows of antipathy.   It was never a sturdy vessel.
Nonetheless the issue of how teaching and research in policy analysis in
Britain should be organised remains with us.   The American experience
can be drawn upon to provide at least a few rudimentary signposts for
the development of policy analysis, and Public Administration in general,
in Britain.

Obviously, Public Administration in Britain has its own distinctive
features.   As is now well understood foreign innovations cannot be
transplanted willynilly if there is to be any expectation of success.
It is just as necessary to locate British developments in their context
as it is American developments.   Accordingly, current developments in
British Public Administration are briefly reviewed before I examine
British experience in teaching Public Administration/policy analysis at

the masters' degree level by presenting a case study of the master's degree programme at the Institute of Local Government Studies, University of Birmingham.

It is not the objective of this monograph to provide a philosophical discussion of the nature of Public Administration/policy analysis, important though this topic may be. In the case of both Britain and the United States, general issues are discussed only in as far as it is a necessary context for the centre-piece of this study - namely, the masters' degree programmes. In all, 5 programmes are discussed and, given their prominence in what follows, it would be as well to indicate how the various case studies were compiled.

I arranged to visit a limited number of universities for a period of approximately one month. By being around and visible for longer than the normal visitor I hoped to provoke a degree of interest in my presence. In addition, I attempted systematically to structure my visit to each university. In the first instance, I collected together the available printed matter on both the school/university and the particular master's degree to ensure that I knew the basics. Second, I attended the core courses on the degree as a means of finding out in more detail what was taught, at what pace and in what manner. Third, I discussed with faculty the courses they taught and sought their opinion on the strengths and weaknesses of the degree as a whole. Fourth, I lectured at nearly all the institutions I visited. Fifth, I saw the deans or directors (and the course administrator if a separate post had been created) to discuss their degree programme and the school in detail. These interviews did not take place until I had been at the university for approximately two weeks and acquired some minimal knowledge of their institution and its work. Last, but by no means least, I talked with the students about their reactions to the degree. Most academics only knew what happened on their own course. The students, however, consumed the degree as a whole. Their comments on the degree of integration between the component courses were especially valuable.

It is perhaps grandiose to describe the above work schedule as a research design but it does indicate that I attempted to become systematically involved in the institutions I visited. My visits were not cursory inspections.

One other aspect of my American schedule should be mentioned. In deciding which universities to visit I attempted to select institutions representing a variety of approaches to the study of Public Administration. The Department of Public Administration, Maxwell School, Syracuse University was chosen as representative of the more traditional approach to Public Administration. The Institute of Public Policy Studies was chosen as representative of the new quantitative approaches to the study of public policy. The Graduate School of Public Policy, University of California (Berkeley) was chosen, and I hope he will forgive me for saying it, because I suspected Aaron Wildavsky would have developed his own distinctive approach to the subject. Finally, I visited the Business School at Stanford University because business schools in general had become major contributors to the study of Public Administration. Although no four universities could possibly represent the full variety of approaches to the study of

Public Administration - for example, I did not pay an extended visit to a health, planning or similar professional school - nonetheless, those chosen do begin to reflect some of that variety.

The British case study has a different origin. From 1973-75, I was the convenor of graduate studies at the Institute of Local Government Studies. The case study is based, therefore, on my own academic teaching over the past few years. I no longer work at the Institute and with the benefit of hindsight, I can offer a critical appraisal of the degree. I am not constrained to defend or justify it. It cannot be claimed that this case study is representative of masters' degrees in Public Administration/policy analysis in Britain. There are few such degree programmes. There are even fewer specifically concerned with policy analysis. The past year has seen the launching of a number of masters' degrees in policy analysis but most have yet to complete their first intake of students. In this situation it can be fairly argued that there are no common yardsticks to guide the choice of case studies. The degree can be viewed as a pioneering venture - it was certainly amongst the first in the field in Britain. It can also be described as a British response to predominantly American intellectual developments.

It is intrinsically interesting, especially for those who work in the particular field, to survey current developments. At worst, it provides a way of checking that ones reading is not too out-of-date. However, this is not the main objective of the present study. The case studies are presented and discussed in the hope that they will inform the development of Public Administration and policy analysis in Britain. This could occur in two ways. First, there is the danger that in following American developments one can copy the faults as well as the virtues. I have tried to identify those aspects of the American experience which could be emulated in Britain. Second, lessons can be learnt about the design of specific courses and the use of specific teaching methods. I have included this kind of detail in the various case studies and in an appendix. Over the next five years there will in all probability be an increase in the number of masters' degree programmes in Public Administration/policy analysis. Such degrees will be all the better for an awareness of the mistakes that others have made. However, this monograph has not been written solely for a British audience. I have also tried to provide a commentary on the current state of Public Administration which will be of interest to American specialists in the field. In particular, it is important to provide an antidote to the strong parochial streak in American Public Administration and the concomitant over-statement of the problems of the subject. Hopefully, the description and discussion of British Public Administration will serve to place many of their so-called 'problems' into clearer perspective.

In brief, the survey of both the intellectual and teaching developments in Britain and the United States explores the following questions:

(a) What are the distinctive features of American Public Administration in the 1970s? (Chapter 2)

(b) To what extent does policy analysis represent a significant new

departure in the study of public bureaucracies?
(Chapter 3)

(c) In what ways do American graduate programmes vary?
(Chapter 4)

(d) What are the distinctive characteristics of British Public
Administration and how has it developed in recent years?
(Chapter 5)

(e) What lessons can be learnt from recent American experience in the
teaching of Public Administration and policy analysis to guide the
future development of British Public Administration?
(Chapter 6)

ACKNOWLEDGEMENTS

This study would not have been possible without the help of a large
number of people.   First and foremost, I must thank Peter Weitz and
the German Marshall Fund of the United States who funded my visit to
the States and thus made it all possible.   Each of the universities
visited accorded me the warmest of welcomes.   And my American
colleagues were, to put it mildly, frank in their assessment of their
degree programmes.   Many of those I talked to wasted little mercy on
the weaknesses of their institutions.   I have tried to retain the
cutting edge and humour of many of my respondents' remarks.   The
occasional colloquialism (and the use of the first person singular)
are normally frowned upon in academic books but they are retained here
in an attempt to capture at least a vestige of the spirit of my many
conversations.   Amongst those responsible for this mood of positive
criticism were Jim Carroll, Jim Garnett and Dwight Waldo of Syracuse
University; Jack Walker at Michigan University; LeRoy Graymer and
Aaron Wildavsky at the University of California (Berkeley); and Henry
Rowen at Stanford University.   To all these individuals, their staff
and students, my grateful thanks.   Although I have been critical of a
number of the masters' degree programmes, I am not repaying kindness
with criticism alone.   No European could fail to be impressed by the
scale of that venture called American Public Administration.   The
criticisms made below should at no time be allowed to obscure this
admiration.   Moreover, it should be remembered that I am discussing
the programmes as they were in 1975.   There can be little doubt that
many changes have occurred since my visit.

Since returning to Britain, I have had the benefit of critical
comments from a number of colleagues.   I would like to thank Richard
Chapman, Andrew Dunsire, Peter Bell, Jim Garnett, Jack Walker, Richard
Baker, Lewis Gunn, Alan Campbell, George Jones, John Stewart and last
but by no means least Dwight Waldo.   They disagreed with much that I
had written but nonetheless encouraged me to continue.   I am grateful
for their help.   As ever, the responsibility for the final text (and
the remaining errors) is mine alone.   Finally, my special thanks to
John Stewart and the Institute of Local Government Studies.   In spite
of a notorious prediliction to insist that there are 54 weeks in a year,
the Institute gave me three months leave of absence.

NOTES AND REFERENCES

1   The decision to concentrate on graduate programmes stemmed in part
    from my own interest in graduate education and also from the
    prominence of graduate programmes in American Public Administration
    teaching.   For a history of the American graduate programmes see
    Alice B. Stone and Donald C. Stone, 'Early Developments of Education
    in American Public Administration' in F.C. Mosher (ed.), American
    Public Administration: past, present, future, University of Alabama
    Press, Alabama, 1975, pp. 11-48 and 268-90.   Undergraduate education
    is not discussed below although it should be noted that it has
    expanded greatly in recent years.   See: National Association of
    Schools of Public Affairs and Administration, Guidelines and
    Standards for Professional Masters' Degree Programs in Public
    Affairs/Public Administration, NASPAA, Washington, D.C., 1974,
    pp.29-30.   Finally, on teaching policy analysis to undergraduates
    see D.G. Smith, Policy Analysis for Undergraduates (A Report to the
    Committee on Public Policy and Social Organisation at the Ford
    Foundation), January 1975.

2   There is a second, and subsidiary, aspect to this labelling problem.
    A distinction can be drawn between the self-conscious study of the
    subject matter and the object of this attention.   Following the
    convention introduced by Dwight Waldo, the practices, processes and
    problems of public bureaucracies are referred to as public
    administration whereas the self conscious study of this subject is
    referred to as Public Administration.

2 The scope of American Public Administration in the 1970s

(i) INTRODUCTION

The history of American Public Administration has been documented so
frequently that it is fair to talk of an orthodoloxy or a conventional
wisdom on the subject.   In brief, it is argued that there has been a
shift from the classical period of the 1930s through a period of
challenge exemplified by the work of Herbert Simon, Robert Dahl and
Dwight Waldo into an era of 'behaviouralism' and especially
organisation theory in the 1960s.(1)   These developments are not
reviewed here.   Attention is focused on American Public Administration
in the 1970s.

Unfortunately there have been few attempts to analyse current
developments and those which do exist are unsatisfactory because of an
obsessive concern with 'the paradigm problem' and the question of whether
Public Administration is a discipline.   As Dwight Waldo has pointed
out the word 'paradigm' has become a '... vogue word used so often and
in so many senses that perhaps it were best to avoid it.'   Waldo
himself uses the term ' ... in the loose sense of "model" or
"pattern" '.(2)   Defining the term 'discipline' is scarcely any easier.
Most commentators would include a discrete subject matter or field of
enquiry, a common pool of theory and concepts, and distinctive methods
of study amongst their defining characteristics.   In addition, one has
to recognise that disciplines are 'social entities' characterised by
the existence of a community of scholars, albeit a diffuse community,
and supported by faculty and departmental forms of organisation within
universities.(3).

Although the terms of the debate are often even less precise than
this brief discussion, nonetheless commentators on Public Administration
are agreed both that it is not a discipline and that this is a problem.
Thus, the literature abounds with assertions such as 'Public
Administration, as an academic discipline, has not carved out a distinct
area of inquiry'.(4)   Waldo talks of ironies, anomalies and a crisis
of identity, arguing in favour of a unifying professional perspective (5)
Ostrom has identified an 'intellectual crisis'.(6)   Schick argues for
a greater involvement of Public Administration with political science.(7)
Nor is this concern of recent origin.(8)   Given the kinds of criteria
mentioned above, the conclusions that Public Administration is not a
discipline and that it lacks a unifying 'paradigm' seem unexceptional.

One response to the lack of disciplinary status has been the attempt
to specify clear disciplinary boundaries.   For example, it has been
argued that organisation theory will provide the requisite synthesis of
the disparate strands encompassed by Public Administration.(9)   In
other words, the important questions in Public Administration appear to
be 'Is it a discipline?' and 'What are the boundaries of Public
Administration?'   But it is perhaps equally important to ask why these
questions are the most important ones and to explore the consequences
of this pre-occupation.

In part the search for disciplinary status reflects a yearning for
the certainties of yesteryear when Public Administration was not so
diffuse.   Another element of a more mundane nature is the fight
against second class citizenship on the part of academics in
departments of Public Administration.   Disciplinary status is the
affirmative action slogan of under-privileged teachers of Public
Administration.   Finally, and perhaps most important, it reflects the
desire to impose intellectual coherence and order onto a complex
subject.   This striving for coherence is an important goal, but it is
not the only goal.   It is important to ask what is being sacrificed
for this coherence.

In describing recent developments in Public Administration, one
feature 'stands out above all others - the diversity of approaches.
Both in terms of recognised disciplines and specific topics, the range
is equally broad.   The problem with that literature which seeks to
define disciplinary boundaries is that it misrepresents this diversity.
It is viewed as a sign of weakness, if not of total disarray.(10)
More appropriate evaluative criteria would seem to be the intellectual
coherence and vigour of the individual approaches and the degree of
debate and competition between them.   In so far as the debate about
the nature of Public Administration promotes debate between the various
approaches, it is playing an invaluable role.   In so far as it
excludes certain approaches and represents diversity as disarray, it
performs a disservice.   In the remainder of this chapter, I attempt to
substantiate the contention that Public Administration is characterised
by a diversity of approaches by describing the varied developments of
the 1970s.   However, before doing so, it is necessary to delimit the
survey to at least some extent by defining the term Public
Administration.

Public Administration is defined as the <u>multi-disciplinary study of</u>
<u>the political-management systems (structures and processes) of public</u>
<u>bureaucracies.</u>   I am under no illusion that this definition will
command agreement but, sacrificing brevity for the sake of some
clarity, it should be discussed in a little more detail.

If Public Administration is not a discipline in the sense of
possessing its own body of theory and methods of study, its
distinctiveness can be said to lie in its subject matter.   The study of
public bureaucracies - or, to use equally common phrases, public
agencies or the machinery of government - is a traditional way of
defining this subject matter.   It refers to the legal (constitutional
and/or customary) definition of public institutions.   It is a
definition that has been criticised for its legalistic nature and
because at the boundary what is, and what is not, a 'public'
institution becomes vague.   In spite of this debate, it is a
definition which provides a clear starting point.   That this core
subject matter can be extended does not mean that the core disappears.
Having located a starting point for Public Administration, it is
necessary to say a little more about the phrase 'public bureaucracies'.
It would be rather unusual to study the colour of the paint on the
windows and doors of such institutions.   Rather, the emphasis is on
public bureaucracies as political-management systems.   The major
reason for joining politics and management is to emphasise the seamless
web of government decision-making.   The initiation of policy, its

7

formulation, promulgation, implementation are interwoven processes.
Public bureaucracies are not exclusively concerned with the application
of received decisions.

The term 'political' is used to draw attention to a number of
features of public bureaucracies. It points to the political
environment within which public bureaucracies operate. In the
decision-making process, political pressures originating from
pressure groups, party politics and public opinion can have a
decisive influence on the final decision. The term emphasises also
that decisions are not only technical but also multi-valued – that a
range of competing values has to be accommodated in any one decision
– and that the public bureaucracies are sources of some of the values
involved in the competition in any decision-making process. Finally,
and by implication, it suggests that the political environment and
the incidence of multi-valued choices are major distinguishing
features of public sector decision-making: thereby suggesting that
public bureaucracies are a distinctive part of that generic area of
study called organisation theory or the sociology of organisations.

The use of the term 'management' draws attention to what are, for
many, the more mundane features of Public Administration. It refers to
the deployment of human, technical and financial resources to achieve
stated ends. The way in which these processes are carried out can
have a crucial effect on the (ostensibly) more important and separate
process of decision-making. Nor is this influence a one-way process.
Managerial processes can themselves be influenced by political
considerations.

The term 'systems' in the phrase political-management systems should
not be ignored. It is used, not to smuggle in a complex terminology
for redescribing the obvious, but to draw attention to the facts that
public bureaucracies are affected by other facets of their environment
than the political aspects and that the component parts of the public
bureaucracy interact with each other.

The terms 'structures and processes' have been included in the
definition for one specific reason. Many early studies of Public
Administration have been criticised for their institutional and legal
focus. Consequently, the emphasis switched to the informal
organisation and to the processes of decision-making rather than the
formal organisation and its procedures. The terms structures and
processes emphasise that Public Administration is concerned with both
aspects.

Finally, this subject matter is the preserve of no one discipline.
Public Administration is a multi-disciplinary subject. Although the
above definition emphasises in places the importance of politics, it
does so because it is an important characteristic of public
bureaucracies and not because it is the only characteristic.

On this view of Public Administration, therefore, there is a
relatively discrete subject matter – the political-management systems
of public bureaucracies – but there is no discipline. Rather the
subject matter is studied from a variety of recognised disciplinary

8

standpoints.   Equally, the subject matter is not the preserve of any
particular school or department.   Public Administration may be a major
focus within a department of economics, a professional school of health
or planning, a department of political science or a department or
school actually labelled Public Administration.   This survey does not
arbitrarily limit the institutional forms through which the subject can
be studied.   And against this backcloth current developments in
American Public Administration are examined.

America's Public Administration, like many other of her social
sciences, is subject to fashions.   Although it is relatively easy to
identify current proccupations, it is slightly more difficult to
determine which, if any, will have any staying-power.   Certainly
developments in Public Administration and policy analysis are
influenced by developments in American government.   In the aftermath
of Watergate there was considerable interest in the problem of
accountability and ethical questions.   Whether these concerns will
survive a less traumatic presidency is a moot point.   Thus to this
foreign observer the 1960s was the era of urban studies, poverty and
participation.   I anticipated that there would still be considerable
activity in these areas.   I was wrong.   Although these topics had
not disappeared, they had definitely slipped into the background
judging by the courses,the contents of their reading lists and the
opinion of faculty at the various universities I visited.   These
criteria are not necessarily definitive, of course.   In one sense,
I am simply reporting on what I read.   However, what I read was
dictated less by my personal interest and more by the expressed
current interests of American academics.   The danger in this approach
is that such interests seem to change very rapidly.   In his 1972
survey of developments in Public Administration, Dwight Waldo noted
poverty, race, urban problems, participation, management techniques,
industrial relations, environmentalism and consumerism as current
challenges to public administration.   Within Public Administration he
noted the move away from political science, the growth of political
economy, public management programmes in business schools, the new
Public Administration and organisational humanism and organisational
development.(11)   A listing in 1976 reveals different emphases,
although there is some overlap.   The impact of unionisation continued
to be felt.   The concern with management techniques persisted.   But
in the post-Watergate era the ethics or political theory of Public
Administration had become very predominant.   Policy analysis or policy
studies emerged as a growth industry.   The concern with organisational
humanism and the new political economy persisted and, equally
important, the preoccupations of Public Administration with defining
the boundaries had revived with the publication of the National
Association of Schools of Public Affairs and Administration (NASPAA)
guidelines and standards for masters' degree programmes.

No short survey of anything as diverse and rapidly changing as
American Public Administration can be comprehensive.   I have selected
four areas for more detailed analysis.   In the rest of this chapter
I briefly describe and comment on organisational humanism,the political
theory of Public Administration and the new political economy.   The
following chapter is devoted exclusively to policy studies.   Of all
the developments considered here, policy studies was indisputably the

most prominent - so much so that, at times, it appeared to be the only significant new focus. By limiting the discussion to these four areas I am not implying that they were equally well developed or that significant research had been carried out in every one of them. They have been selected because they were foci of attention at the time of my visit and not because of their outstanding merit or significant achievements.

(ii)   ORGANISATIONAL HUMANISM

For much of the post-war period organisation theory has been a thriving area of academic concern which has taken a variety of directions.(12) There have been many developments over the past two decades. At the time of my visit to America, however, organisational humanism was a very prominent strand within organisation theory. The relationship between the individual and the organisation has been, of course, a recurrent topic throughout much of the post-war period. Organisational humanism is simply the most recent stage in the development of research in the area. Its focus is the individual within organisations and its concern is to democratise organisations and thereby increase the opportunities for self realisation. Its leading exponents are well known - Maslow, Likert, McGregor, Argyris and Bennis - as are many of the techniques - e.g.T-groups, group building, sensitivity training.(13) Paradoxically, in spite of the long standing interest in the topic and its fashionable status, the contribution of organisational humanism to Public Administration was a potential rather than an actual contribution. There were virtually no studies applying organisational humanism to public bureaucracies, (14) although it was a major area of interest.

The 'patron saint' of organisational humanism, Abraham Maslow, can be classed as an organisational humanist only with some difficulty. Nonetheless, his hierarchy of needs has been extensively employed and it occupies the same status in organisational humanism as Weber's ideal type of bureaucracy does in the study of organisational structures. Maslow argues that human needs are organised in a hierarchy of importance from physiological needs through safety, belongingness and esteem to self actualising needs. As soon as one need in the hierarchy is satisfied, the next emerges. Self actualisation is the key concept. It is defined by Maslow as follows:

> 'A musician must make music, an artist must paint, a poet must write if he is to be ultimately at peace with himself. What a man can be, he must be. He must be true to his own nature. This need we may call self actualisation.'(15)

Subsequent theories have been concerned to develop ways and means whereby the employee's work situation supports the drive for autonomy and self expression rather than frustrates it. Although individual happiness is an important reason for introducing new management structures, styles and techniques, it is not the sole reason. It is argued also that the self actualising employee is more productive. In other words, individual and organisational goals are congruent. In the search for more supportive management structures, much interest has focused on matrix organisation - a structure composed of problem-centred,

multi-specialist groups which are created and dissolved as problems
arise and are dispensed with. (16)   Warren Bennis has argued that, in
an era of ever more rapid change - of turbulent environments -
organisations need to evolve highly flexible structures to cope with
change.   Bureaucracy is seen as mechanistic and inflexible. Organic
adaptive structures are required in its place(17) - 'Ad-hocracy', to
use Toffler's term. (18)   Organisational humanism is not just,
therefore, an impassioned pleas for the rights of the individual in
the organisational society, it is also a grand design for
democratising and restructuring organisations.

There is a third component.   Perhaps because of organisational
humanism's heavy emphasis on individual autonomy and self expression,
behavioural methods of study are criticised for ignoring the emotional,
the valuational and the perceptual aspects of knowing.   Stated baldly,
the individual interprets and defines his own situation within the
organisation and in order to understand the organisation the researcher must
understand these definitions of the situation.   Not only is the
individual's perception of his work situation crucial to understanding
organisations but it is inadequately captured by attitude questionnaires
and the researcher in the role of detached observer.   The researcher
must involve himself in the work situation so that he can perceive it
through the eyes of the employee.   But in so doing, the researcher
alters the work situation.   He is not invisible.   He must comprehend,
therefore, that he is studying not only the interactions of his
'subjects' but that he is a subject also and he must study his own
actions and reactions as they affect both himself and others.   In
contrast to more orthodox strategies, self knowledge and subjective
knowledge are accorded a high priority. (19)

Organisational humanism has raised a number of questions for the
study of Public Administration.   Such questions concern personnel
management, relations with clients, and management structures.   How
can reforms aimed at increasing employee autonomy - participative
management - be reconciled with the political accountability of
elected representatives and officials?   How can parity of treatment
continue to be accorded to all clients if each client is seen as a
unique individual?   How are professional career hierarchies reconciled
with matrix groups whose membership accords greater importance to
expertise than seniority?   In posing these questions, I am not
suggesting that they invalidate the claims of organisational humanism.
I am simply attempting to demonstrate that, in spite of the
evangelical tone of much of the literature and the limited application
to public bureaucracies, organisational humanism does raise highly
practical issues - issues which have been surmounted in a number of
industrial settings.

Organisational humanism has a number of distinctive and practical
features.   It has an appeal well beyond the confines of academia.   It
is a cake baked from a mixture of existential philosophy and radical
ideology, sprinkled with a range of careful empirical studies, packaged
in a variety of research strategies and techniques and sold through a
massive advertising campaign.   The problem is to separate the useful
and insightful from the more ephemeral aspects.

The claims of organisational humanism at the level of employee motivation have not remained undisputed. As Alan Fox has pointed out:

'Maslow, more cautious than many of his disciples, stresses the "shaky foundations" of his self actualisation propositions; suggests that their validity may well be limited to certain kinds of culture and certain types of personality structure; and emphasises the need for more research'.(20)

Nor is work self-evidently a means for realising individual potential. C.Wright Mills has pointed out that:

'Work may be a mere source of livelihood, or the most significant part of one's inner self; it may be experienced as expiation, or an exuberant expression of self; as bounden duty, or as the development of man's universal nature. Neither love nor hatred of work is inherent in man, or inherent in any given line of work. For work has no intrinsic meaning'. (my emphasis) (21)

Perrow, in reviewing much of the literature in the area, comments that 'tested ideas are hard to come by', suggests that many of the changes attributed to changes in management style can be more plausibly explained by other factors (e.g. changes in the structure), and concludes that:

' ... there is little empirical support for the human relations theory or theories, that extensive efforts to find that support have resulted in increasing limitations and contingencies, and that the grand schemes such as Likert's appear to be methodo-logically unsound and theoretically biased ... One cannot explain organisations by explaining the attitudes of individuals or even small groups within them. We learn a great deal about psychology and social psychology but little about organisations per se in this fashion'.(22)

Reservations have been expressed also about the 'intervention strategies' associated with organisational humanism. It has been claimed that they are manipulative, trying to mould the individual to fit organisational requirements. But a far more important question than the criticisms noted so far - and they are criticisms not to be dismissed lightly - concerns the underlying socio-political theory.

The application of the ideas of organisational humanism to public bureaucracies, if and when it occurs, is likely to face some important problems. It is argued that the challenge to government from its environment requires it to replace the existing mechanistic structures with adaptive- organic structures. These structures are usually composed of ad hoc, project or problem-oriented groups characterised by non-directive leadership. In this way, the new structures of government and individual needs become congruent. The individual seeks autonomy and self expression which can be achieved in project groups. Government needs to cope with rapid change and can do so through the introduction of adaptive, group based structures. In Warren Bennis' phrase 'Democracy is inevitable'.(23) But what, one may enquire, happened to politics? It has been defined out of existence. Government is just one type of organisation amongst many large organisations. The 'polity' has been fragmented into a series of organisational constituencies. The new leadership styles in these organisations substitute consensus for coercion or compromise in the management of conflict. Influence is based on technical competence and knowledge and not on 'the vagaries of personal whims or prerogatives of power'. In the words of one critic, this is the 'sublimation of politics', and the new leaders are 'cut to truly classic proportions'. (24)

Setting down the underlying socio-political theory in this bald way prompts some questions. If it is agreed that twentieth century western society is dominated by large organisations, does it follow that each organisation should be viewed as a separate polity? Sheldon Wolin poses the issue starkly:

' "Political" responsibility has meaning only in terms of a general constituency, and no multiplication of fragmentary constituencies will provide a substitute. Similarly, to contend that individual participation can be satisfied in a political way within the confines of non-political groups is to deprive citizenship of its meaning and to render political loyalty impossible.

... citizenship provides what the other roles cannot, namely an integrative experience which brings together the multiple role-activities of the contemporary person and demands that the separate roles be surveyed from a more general point of view.' (25)

This discussion of organisational humanism has been brief and it has not distinguished between a number of writers who are, at best, uneasy bedfellows. Nonetheless, the general themes discussed are common to many, if not all of these writers. The emphasis on self actualisation and the sublimation of politics recurs throughout much of the literature. The perspective is a distinctive one, challenging as it does accepted canons on employee behaviour and the meaning of such terms as political responsibility and citizenship. At the end of the day, however, it is a view which must be judged narrow, if not outright reductionist. The focus cannot remain internal to organisations. The impact of such organisations on each other, on society, and the impact of society on organisations are topics of key importance which the micro-perspective of organisational humanism tends to ignore. They are topics which reintroduce the grand themes of political theory - the public interest, political responsibility, the nature of citizenship.

(iii)   POLITICAL THEORY IN PUBLIC ADMINISTRATION

The impact of the Watergate scandal on American society has been enormous and for Public Administration has led to an increased concern with the ethics and the political theory of public administration. (26) Such approaches in Public Administration are not new (27) but they have been peripheral concerns in the past. Post-Watergate, they moved to

13

the centre of the stage. As with organisational humanism, however, it is difficult to identify a coherent body of literature on ethics and political theory centrally concerned with public bureaucracies. Dwight Waldo has pointed to the literature on anarchy, feudalism, stateless societies and democracy as 'suggestive'. (28) It is not necessary to range quite so broadly. One specific manifestation of the concern with ethics and political theory can be used to illustrate this development - namely, the new Public Administration. The major problem facing anyone wishing to describe the new Public Administration is yet again the sheer diffuseness of the development. The two major volumes (29) on the topic encompass such a diversity of views that common denominators are hard to identify. Marini suggests the following characteristics:

(a) relevance, to both current problems and the practitioner;

(b) post-positivism and a break from value free or value neutral research;

(c) adapting to turbulence in the environment; and

(d) developing new organisational forms concerned with involvement, openness, personal morality and clients. (30)

If these characteristics seem somewhat general and by no means limited to the new Public Administration, the reader has probably grasped the most important point about this aspect of Public Administration. Moreover, a number of writers included in the Marini and Waldo volumes give no obvious evidence of supporting any of these tenets! The problem of diffuseness is further compounded by lack of follow-up writing and research which could clarify the original position. The new Public Administration was in large measure simply an event.

A distinction has been drawn between the study of Public Administration and the institutional form through which it is studied. The new Public Administration is, in large measure, the response of the 'discipline' or departments of Public Administration to the ferment elsewhere in the study of 'their' subject. It is not surprising, therefore, that these other developments - for example, organisational humanism - formed a substantial part of the proceedings. Apart from noting that the new Public Administration is an exercise in self assertion by the discipline, the event has had one important effect. By drawing together, but by no stretch of the imagination integrating, the various aspects in Public Administration at two conferences and in two collections of papers, the event contributed to the intellectual climate. It stimulated interest, created debate and spread awareness of the diversity of approaches to the study of Public Administration. In Waldo's phrase it was a 'yeasty addition' and for this it should be accorded due credit.

It is a second aspect of the proceedings which is of particular relevance here, however, although it is limited to only some of the contributors to the new Public Administration. This is the attempt to consider the role of the bureaucrat normatively - what role ought the bureaucrat to adopt? In brief, the claim is made that social science

14

can never be value free and, consequently, Public Administration should openly avow and serve the values of social justice and social equality. Public Administration should strive to protect the deprived. And in so doing:

> '... it may be necessary for the new Public Administration
> to develop outside of the existing institutional framework
> and thinking of the university and government.' (31)

Public Administration should prepare 'guerrillas in the bureaucracy' or 'short-haired radicals'. The concern with the intrusion of values into 'objective' social research; the prevalence of poverty and discrimination in American society; the influence of organisational humanism and its anti-hierarchic sentiments; and the concern for clients have coalesced into a search for a new kind of public morality - in this case a radical ethic. Victor Thompson, in an intemperate response to the new Public Administration, comments:

> 'This viewpoint represents a most amazing effort to establish
> a new claimant in place of the owner (that is, in place of the
> public). It is a brazen attempt to 'steal' the popular sovereignty.
> ... Aside from the political absurdity and immaturity of
> this program, it would not solve the problem of compassion
> for the poor and downtrodden, and it would leave all the
> rest of us, the vast majority, with our problem unsolved...'(32)

If the active espousal of such radical views did pervade the new Public Administration, Thompson's case would be stronger. In fact, it is but one theme among many and a minority view at that. But even worse, Thompson misses the point, which is the increasing concern with political theory shown by many of the contributors to the new Public Administration without committing themselves to any particular political stance. Thompson insists on putting forward as conclusions matters which were of unresolved debate. Presumably he would not deny that Public Administration can encompass questions of justice and equality. This simple fact of concern with political values and their relationship to Public Administration is significant. It is probably the lasting contribution of the new Public Administration out of all their diverse subjects. Unfortunately this concern has borne little fruit as yet in writing and research. Waldo and Wolin still remain the major contributors to the political theory of Public Administration. The political theory of Public Administration remains as yet an unfulfilled promise.

The new Public Administration is less a continuing intellectual force in Public Administration and more a stimulating event which both brought together in one place many disparate views and, most importantly, reasserted the relevance of political theory to the subject. The agenda of the new Public Administration supplements traditional topics such as the structural characteristics of organisation, budgeting and co-ordination with moral precepts and principles emphasising clients, public morality, and the replacement of hierarchies. (33)

Economists have played an increasingly prominent role in the study of
Public Administration and, as will become clear in the next chapter, in
the development of policy analysis. At this juncture I explore that
contribution which has stemmed not from their subject matter and
specific technical skills but from their characteristic method of
analysis. The economist's method has been described as follows:

> 'He will postulate the existence of a number of individual
> actors, with certain ends (such as maximising their income),
> and will then try to work out deductively how they will act
> in a situation of a kind which presents certain alternatives
> to them, on the assumption that they pursue their goals
> rationally.' (34)

This hypothetico-deductive approach can be seen as a theory of
rational behaviour, and, in recent years, it has been applied to the
study of bureaucracy. For example, Downs postulates that 'bureaucratic
officials ... are significantly ... motivated by their own self-
interests and that they 'seek to attain their goals rationally.' (35)
He then uses his central axiom to derive a series of propositions
about bureaucratic behaviour. The same method is employed by Tullock
and Niskanen. (36) The methods are those of micro-economics, the
focus is the behaviour of the individual bureaucrat.

It should not be thought, however, that all studies utilising the
economic approach focus solely on the individual bureaucrat. Ostrom
uses the approach to review the inadequacies of conventional
administrative theory. (37) Bish reviews the literature on metropolitan areas to demonstrate the utility of the economic approach,and
there are many other examples of the use of the economic approach on
non-economic subject matter. (38) I do not propose to review this
body of literature in its entirety - the exercise has been carried out
already by Brian Barry. However, the studies of bureaucracy by Downs,
Niskanen and Tullock were not singled out for attention in Barry's
survey and they are oft-cited and used as textbooks in Public
Administration programmes. In the context of this survey of American
Public Administration, therefore, it is particularly relevant to
examine their contributions. It will enable me to discuss an
important development in American Public Administration without undue
repetition.

The first point to be considered concerns the plausibility of the
premises used in the economic approach. Clearly to anyone familiar
with organisation theory the assumptions about self interest and
rational choice would have to be very heavily qualified, even discarded,
if they were supposed to be descriptive of individual behaviour in large
organisations. Simon's administrative man supplanted economic man as
a description of actual behaviour nearly thirty years ago. The
premises are not, however, meant to be descriptively accurate. They do
not even have to be plausible. It is argued that the criterion of
their adequacy is the testability of the hypotheses they generate.
There are two aspects to this claim. First, the hypotheses thus

generated cannot simply be plausible. It has to be possible to refute
them. It is an eminently unsatisfactory procedure, for example, to
put forward descriptively unrealistic premises about human motivation
to deduce hypotheses of human behaviour which can only be tested by
imputing motives to the observed behaviour. It follows also that the
hypothesis should be to some degree non-obvious - i.e. should throw new
light on the subject. Unfortunately these defects are not always
conspicuous by their absence. Consider just one example from the long
list of hypotheses suggested by Downs (and many more could be added):

'Inequalities of power, income and prestige are greater
in tall hierarchies than in flat ones.' (39)

First, hierarchies by definition are grading devices designed to
create inequalities. Consequently, the greater the number of
gradations the greater the inequality between the extremes. Second,
the inclusion of the concept of power as a commodity, the unequal
distribution of which can be measured, suggests that testing this
hypothesis may be difficult. Third, Downs himself admits that 'it is
not always clear precisely how each proposition could actually be
tested.' Fourth, it is not the most startling of insights.

Finally, many of the hypotheses are false. For example, Downs hypo-
thesises that control is dependent upon the superior's ability to
influence the promotion of subordinates. (40) But control is
exercised in a variety of ways and authority has various legitimating
bases. Command over sanctions is but one form of control and it may
not be the most important, let alone appropriate form. Moreover, the
hypothesis itself assumes self interest on the part of the subordinate
and superior. How one refutes this motivational base of control and
compliance without imputing different motives to the observed behaviour
of the actors is a difficult problem.

To this point the discussion has focused on the testability, not the
actual testing, of hypotheses. If the economic approach is to
demonstrate its utility, testable hypotheses by themselves are inadequate.
Such hypotheses must also be tested. Unfortunately, anecdotes prevail
over field research. Niskanen comments:

'Although I bring personal observations and casual evidence to
bear in support of several of the behavioural hypotheses,
this book does not present the set of critical tests necessary to
confirm ... this theory.'(41)

This statement is common. As an intellectual exercise, the economic
approach can be great fun but ultimately hypotheses must be generated
and tested. The studies being discussed in this section leave a lot
to be desired in the generation of precisely formulated, non-obvious
hypotheses which can be, and are, tested. If one moves away from
studies of bureaucracy to other areas such as locational choices or a
pure theory of local expenditures where the attempt has been made to
test the hypotheses generated, the fate of the economic approach has
not been a happy one. Tiebout, Ostrom et al. (42) hypothesised that
local residents acted as customers moving from locality to locality
until they obtained that combination of local services and tax rates

in accord with their preferences. Presumably the economic approach is
intended to be of universal applicability. This raises the question
of how British residents could choose their own mix of services when
those services were provided by one authority and not by a profusion
of single function districts with overlapping but not coterminous
boundaries. Ignoring this difficulty, however, and remaining firmly
in the USA, Williams has reviewed the available evidence on locational
choices and he concludes, 'Many studies of why people move fail to
support the economic market hypothesis.'(43)

Definitionally true hypotheses, hypotheses cast in untestable form,
hypotheses which ignore available evidence, the lack of tests, and the
failure of the few available research studies to support the hypotheses.
do not necessarily invalidate the economic approach. It does suggest,
however, that a little more care could be taken in presenting the case
for its use. If self interest and rational choice are axioms with
considerable explanatory power in the study of bureaucratic behaviour,
this has to be demonstrated, especially in view of the large number of
empirical studies which do not use, and deny the validity of, self
interest as a cause of the observed behaviour. As Self notes:

> ' ... the explanation of administrative competition and
> aggrandisement within American government can be traced
> to institutional and political factors, rather than the
> egoistic ambitions of officials.'(44)

To counterbalance this conclusion, it is worth while noting Brian
Barry's general assessment of the economic approach, that it:

> ' ... can permit the production of theories which yield
> genuine predictions when their assumptions are satisfied.'(45)

He recognises that many situations are too complex for the approach,
that premises cannot be derived which will yield determinate solutions.
Perhaps bureaucratic behaviour is one of those situations.

(v)   CONCLUSIONS

Public Administration in America is a thriving subject. Its one
dominating characteristic during the post-war period has been its
eclecticism and the attendant debates between the various approaches to
the subject. Out of this debate has emerged much scholarly work and
yet the picture painted of the subject by American commentators is too
often one of unrelieved gloom. To this observer such gloom seems to
be a classic instance of not seeing the wood for the trees. There are
many trees, but because they do not form a clearly circumscribed forest
it is claimed that no forest exists. Such an argument seems inadequate.
The study of public administration has probably become one of the most
important areas of academic endeavour over the past decade. This fact
should be given prominence and not the absence of neat and tidy
boundaries.

Obviously the full diversity of American Public Administration has not
been described. The development of organisation theory has been noted

but not discussed in any detail. The rise of urban studies, participation, poverty, race, labour relations, management techniques, environmentalism and consumerism as issues of concern during the 1960s have similarly only been noted. Moreover, this is to ignore the more traditional areas of concern - e.g. budgeting, inter-governmental relations. But these omissions to one side, the descriptions presented of organisational humanism, the political theory of public administration and the new political economy should have illustrated the diversity of American Public Administration. Another commentator on his own visit to America may select different areas as ones of current concern. It is unlikely, however, that he will find uniformity of interests and concerns among students of Public Administration.

Diversity of itself has little virtue if the individual components are valueless. I have tried to show, however, that each approach has its merits. Organisational humanism challenges accepted canons about employee motivation and the definition of such terms as political responsibility. The new Public Administration spread awareness of the various approaches and stimulated the re-awakening interest in political theory. Micro-economics has brought a distinctive approach to the subject matter which challenges the more prevalent research strategies. Each approach may have its limitations but, equally important, each has made a contribution to the understanding of public bureaucracies.

Against this backcloth and in the face of that complexity termed public bureaucracies, the plea for integration seems to call for nothing less than a comprehensive theory of the relationship between government and society. Issues such as the relationship between bureaucracies and clients, the rationality of government decision-making, and the values espoused in public administration, all raise questions of far-reaching significance. Such questions are not new nor are they 'little local difficulties'. To quote John Gaus' dictum of 1950, 'a theory of public administration means in our time a theory of politics also'.(46) The search for integrating theories or a 'paradigm' will continue, of course, but given the enormity of the task it seems unreasonable to predicate developments in Public Administration on the arrival of a 'paradigm'. It is more important to test current orthodoxies of both practitioner and academic, to explore unstudied areas and to develop research skills.

As indicated earlier, policy analysis or policy studies is perhaps the major development in Public Administration of recent years. One writer has gone so far as to claim that 'Public Administration is public policy-making'.(47) Before suggesting any more conclusions about the state of American Public Administration in the mid-1970s, it would be as well to examine this particular development.

NOTES AND REFERENCES

(1)   For general discussions of the development of American Public
      Administration see J.C.Charlesworth (ed.), <u>Theory and Practice of</u>
      <u>Public Administration</u>, The American Academy of Political and Social
      <u>Science</u>, Philadelphia, 1968; K.M.Henderson, <u>Emerging Synthesis in</u>
      <u>American Public Administration</u>, Asia Publishing House, London, 1966;

and F.C.Mosher (ed.), <u>American Public Administration: past, present future</u>, University of Alabama Press, Alabama, 1975. The seminal contributions on this topic have come from Dwight Waldo. See D. Waldo, <u>The Administrative State</u>, Ronald Press, New York, 1948; D. Waldo, 'Public Administration', <u>Journal of Politics</u> (30) 1968: pp.443-79; and D. Waldo, 'Developments in Public Administration'. <u>The Annals of the American Academy of Political and Social Science</u> (404) 1972: pp.217-45.

(2)   D. Waldo, 'Education for Public Administration in the Seventies', in Mosher (ed.), <u>American Public Administration</u>, pp.222-23.

(3)   This discussion barely introduces a complex topic. Some of these complexities are brought out in W.J.M.Mackenzie, <u>The Study of Political Science Today</u>, Macmillan, London, 1970, Ch.2. The term 'social entities' is taken from Mackenzie, p.21.

(4)   Henderson, <u>Emerging Synthesis in American Public Administration</u>, p.45. For a recent example of a textbook preoccupied with 'the paradigm problem' see N.Henry, <u>Public Administration and Public Affairs</u>, Prentice Hall, Englewood Cliffs, N.J., 1975.

(5)   D. Waldo, 'Scope of the Theory of Public Administration', in Charlesworth (ed.), <u>Theory and Practice of Public Administration</u>, pp. 1-26.

(6)   V.Ostrom, <u>The Intellectual Crisis in American Public Administration</u>, University of Alabama Press, Alabama, 1973.

(7)   A.Schick, 'The Trauma of Politics: Public Administration in the Sixties', in Mosher (ed.), <u>American Public Administration</u>, pp.142-80.

(8)   For a listing of additional reviews of Public Administration in the post-war period see J.W.Fesler, 'Public Administration and the Social Sciences: 1946-1960', in Mosher (ed.), <u>American Public Administration</u>, pp.140-41.

(9)   Henderson, <u>Emerging Synthesis in American Public Administration</u>, Ch.3. Alternatively, Ostrom has argued in favour of micro-economic theory as the unifying perspective.

(10)   For example, see Schick, 'The Trauma of Politics ...', p.156.

(11)   Waldo, 'Developments in Public Administration', pp.222-41.

(12)   There have been many surveys of the development of organisation theory. Perhaps the most comprehensive of these is J.G.March (ed.), <u>Handbook of Organisations</u>, Rand McNally, New York, 1965. An interesting view from the 'discipline' of Public Administration is D.Waldo, 'Organisation Theory: an elephantine problem', <u>Public Administration Review</u> (21) 1961: pp.210-25.

(13)   For example, see A.Maslow, <u>Motivation and Personality</u>, Harper and Row, New York, 1961; D.McGregor, <u>The Human Side of Enterprises</u>, McGraw Hill, New York, 1960; C.Argyris, <u>Personality and Organisation</u>, Harper and Row, New York, 1957; C.Argyris, <u>Integrating the Individual and the Organisation</u>, Wiley, New York, 1964; and W.G.Bennis, <u>Changing Organisations</u>, McGraw Hill, New York, 1966.

(14)   However, organisational humanism has had a pervasive effect on the new Public Administration. For example, see F.Marini (ed.), <u>Toward a New Public Administration</u>, Chandler, Scranton, Pennsylvania, 1971. In addition, see R.T.Golembiewski, <u>Men, Management and Morality</u>, McGraw Hill, New York, 1965; L.Kirkhart, 'The Future of Organisational Development', <u>Public Administration Review</u> (34) 1974: pp.129-39, and O.F.White, Jr., 'The Dialectical Organisation: an

alternative to bureaucracy', Public Administration Review (29) 1969:
pp.32-42.
(15)   Maslow, Motivation and Personality, p.46.
(16)   On matrix or project organisation see D.I. Cleland and W.R.King,
Systems Analysis and Project Management, McGraw Hill, New York, 1968.
(17)   Bennis, Changing Organisations, pp.12-13.
(18)   A.Toffler, Future Shock, Pan Books, London, 1971, p.120.
(19)   The literature on this point is very diffuse, but see C.Hampden-
Turner, Radical Man, Doubleday, New York, 1971; P.L.Berger and T.Luck-
man, The Social Construction of Reality, Doubleday, New York, 1966;
C. Wilson, Introduction to the New Existentialism, Houghton Mifflin,
Boston, 1967; D. Silverman, The Theory of Organisations, Heineman,
London, 1970; and M.Rose, Industrial Behaviour, Allen Lane, The
Penguin Press, London, 1975, Chs. 25-30.   There is also a 'popular'
literature concerned with the issue of self-realisation.   For example,
see C. Reich, The Greening of America, Penguin Books, Harmondsworth,
1971; R.M.Pirsig, Zen and the Art of Motorcycle Maintenance, Bantam
Books, New York, 1975; and C.Castenada, The Teachings of Don Juan,
Pocket Books, New York, 1974.
(20)   A.Fox, A Sociology of Work in Industry, Collier-Macmillan, London,
1971, p.6.   Fox is quoting from A.H.Maslow, Eupsychian Management,
Irwin and the Dorsey Press, Homewood, Illinois, 1965.
(21)   C.Wright Mills, White Collar, Oxford University Press, New York,
1956, p.215.
(22)   C. Perrow, Complex Organisations, Scott, Foresman,Glenview, Ill.,
1972, p.143.   For a reply to Perrow and other critics see C.Argyris,
The Applicability of Organisational Sociology, Cambridge University
Press, London, 1972.
(23)   W.G.Bennis and P.E.Slater, The Temporary Society, Harper and Row,
New York, 1969, Ch.1.
(24)   S.Wolin, Politics and Vision, Little Brown, Boston, 1960., Ch. 10 .
The quote is from p.423.
(25)   Wolin, Politics and Vision, pp.433-34.
(26)   On the implications for Public Administration of Watergate see
F.C.Mosher (ed.), Watergate: the implications for responsible government, Basic Books, New York, 1974.
(27)   For example see Waldo, The Administrative State; and Wolin,
Politics and Vision.
(28)   D. Waldo, 'Reflections on Public Morality', a lecture sponsored
by the Maxwell School of Citizenship and Public Affairs in conjunction
with the annual meeting of the American Society for Public Administration, Syracuse, May 1974.
(29)   Marini, Toward a New Public Administration; and D. Waldo (ed.),
Public Administration in a Time of Turbulence, Chandler, Scranton,
Penn., 1971.   The Public Administration Review (34) No.1, January/
February 1974 was devoted to a discussion of the new Public Administration.
(30)   F.Marini, 'The Minnowbrook Perspective and the Future of Public
Administration Education', in Marini, Toward a New Public Administration, pp.348-52.
(31)   Bob Zimring, 'Comment: Empirical Theory and the New Public
Administration', in Marini, Toward a New Public Administration, p.233.
(32)   V.Thompson, Without Sympathy or Enthusiasm, University of Alabama
Press, Alabama, 1975, p.66.
(33)   See also K.Henderson,'American Public Administration in the Age

of Aquarius', <u>Public Administration Bulletin</u>, No.10, June 1971, pp. 7-17.

(34) B.Barry, <u>Economists, Sociologists and Democracy</u>, Collier-Macmillan, London, 1970, p.5.

(35) A.Downs, <u>Inside Bureaucracy</u>, Little, Brown, Boston, 1967, p.2.

(36) See G.Tullock, <u>The Politics of the Bureaucracy</u>, Public Affairs Press, Washington D.C., 1965; and W.Niskanen, <u>Bureaucracy and Representative Government</u>, Aldine-Atherton, Chicago, 1971.

(37) Ostrom, <u>The Intellectual Crisis</u>...

(38) R.L.Bish, <u>The Public Economy of Metropolitan Area</u>, Markham, Chicago, 1971. Other examples of this approach include G.Tullock, <u>Private Wants, Public Means: an economic analysis of the desirable scope of government</u>, Basic Books, New York, 1970; G.Wamsley and M.Zald, <u>The Political Economy of Public Organisations</u>, D.C.Heath, Lexington, Mass., 1973; and V.Ostrom and E.Ostrom, 'Public Choice: a different approach to the study of Public Administration', <u>Public Administration Review</u> (31) 1971: pp.203-16.

(39) Downs, <u>Inside Bureaucracy</u>, p.265.

(40) Downs, <u>Inside Bureaucracy</u>, p.267.

(41) Niskanen, <u>Bureaucracy and Representative Government</u>, p.8. For a critique of Niskanen see R.E.Goodin, 'Possessive Individualism Again' <u>Political Studies</u> (24) 1976: pp.488-501.

(42) C.M.Tiebout, 'A Pure Theory of Local Expenditures', <u>Journal of Political Economy</u> (64) 1956: pp.416-24; and V.Ostrom, C.E. Tiebout and R. Warren, 'The Organisation of Government in Metropolitan Areas: a theoretical inquiry', <u>American Political Science Review</u>(55) 1961: pp.831-42.

(43) O. Williams, <u>Metropolitan Political Analysis</u>, The Free Press, New York, 1971, p.56.

(44) P.Self, <u>Administrative Theories and Politics</u>, Allen and Unwin, London, 1972, p.236. Criticisms of the public choice literature can be found in R.T. Golembiewski, 'A Critique of "Democratic Administration" and its Supporting Ideation', <u>American Political Science Review</u> (71) 1977: pp.1488-1507, along with a response from Vincent Ostrom (pp.1508-25) and a rejoinder by Golembiewski (pp.1526-31). An early but still very pertinent critique can be found in B. Barry, <u>Political Argument</u>, Routledge and Kegan Paul, London, 1965. See also Goodin, 'Possessive Individualism Again'.

(45) Barry, <u>Economists, Sociologists and Democracy</u>, p.180.

(46) Quoted in Waldo, 'Scope of the Theory of Public Administration', p.14.

(47) W.H.Lambright, 'The Minnowbrook Perspective and the Future of Public Affairs: Public Administration is Public Policy-Making', in Marini, <u>Toward a New Public Administration</u>, p.332.

3 A rose by any other name: the search for Policy Analysis

(i)   INTRODUCTION

The trouble with products emblazoned with the slogan 'new' is that,
under the packaging, the product is remarkably similar to earlier
products.   By common consent, the revival in the study of public
policy-making was inaugurated by Daniel Lerner and Harold Lasswell in
1951 in their Policy Sciences.(1)   It was not until the late 1960s
and the 1970s, however, that interest in this 'new' area became marked.
What is this new product?   What are the differences between policy
studies and policy analysis?   In the 1960s Dwight Waldo described the
growth industry of that decade, organisation theory, as an elephantine
problem.(2)   In the 1970s, the subject matter has changed but the
proportions of the problem have remained constant.(3)

A fairly obvious starting-point for a discussion of public policy-
making is with definitions.   Presumably the various proponents of this
new field of study are able to say what it is.   Unfortunately, there
is as much disagreement as there is agreement.   For E.S. Quade:

' ... policy analysis may be defined as any type of analysis
that generates and presents information in such a way as to
improve the basis for policy-makers to exercise their judgement.'(4)

The utility of information for the policy-maker does not figure in
Thomas Dye's definition:

'Policy analysis is the description and explanation of the
causes and consequences of government activity.'(5)

On the other hand, Harold Lasswell tries to encompass the positions
adopted by both Quade and Dye.   He suggests that:

'Policy sciences are concerned with knowledge of and in
the decision processes of the public and civic order.'(6)

And if this definition appears to be insufficiently ambitious, the
following definition should redress the balance:

' ... public policy analysis is a future-oriented inquiry
into the optimum means of achieving a given set of social
objectives.'(7)

Finally, to close on a more modest and iconoclastic note, Aaron
Wildavsky defines policy analysis in the following terms:

'Policy analysis is an art form.   Its subjects are problems
that must tentatively be solved before they can be understood
... Nothing is more stultifying than a futile search for
Aristotelian essences that starts with "I don't know either,
but it must be around somewhere" '.(8)

And all of the above definitions have the advantage of brevity. They can extend over several pages.(9)

Public policy-making can mean many things to many men if not quite all things to all men. The above definitions do no more than indicate some of the variety which is subsumed under the label public policy-making. If we are to identify what is new about the study of public policy-making a second line of attack is called for. The various forms which this development takes need to be classified. Figure 3:1 presents such a classification.

The various categories in Figure 3:1 differ in the degree to which they are concerned with providing analysis <u>for</u> policy and to which they are concerned with the analysis of policy. Or, to employ a familiar terminology, policy analysis is prescriptive whereas policy studies is primarily descriptive. This disjunction between prescription and description runs throughout the study of public policy-making. However, the extent of the agreement on the use of terms should not be over-stated. Similar distinctions to those in Figure 3:1 are essential for the discussion to proceed, but the particular terms employed are only one way of characterising the variety of approaches to the study of public policy-making.

The major characteristic of policy analysis is its concern to provide information, analysis and advice which is geared to the improvement of policies and policy-making. Although the description and explanation of the causes and consequences of government activity is not proscribed, it is only carried out in so far as it is relevant to making prescriptions. There are, of course, many differences in emphasis within this broad rubric. Such work can be carried out in a university department or institute, in an independent research institute or within public bureaucracies. The kind of work can range from advocating a particular policy or set of policies, through the collection of useful information and the provision of advice on alternative policies, to the retrospective evaluation of policies either with a view to assessing their effectiveness or to designing new policies.

In marked contrast, policy studies does not stress the utility of research for the policy-maker. Rather output studies attempt to explain the patterns of expenditure of public bureaucracies and considerable emphasis has fallen on the influence of socio-economic variables in the determination of policy. Studies of policy content have had a narrower focus. Their concern has been to study a particular policy, how it has operated and its effects. The studies carried out within the broad rubric of policy studies may be of use to the policy-maker as in the case of retrospective evaluations of the effectiveness of policies, but this is not the prime objective of such work.

Quite clearly, this description of the various guises of public policy-making is brief. The intention is not to detail the variety but simply to draw attention to its very existence. In itself, this step is important. For example, it is claimed that public policy-making is 'new'. However, if one evaluates this claim against the above characterisation of public policy-making in all its guises, a degree of

24

FIGURE 3:1

VARIETIES OF PUBLIC POLICY-MAKING

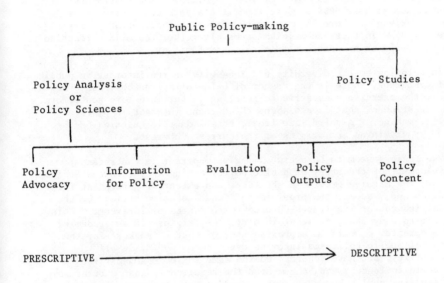

Adapted from: Ian Gordon, Janet Lewis and Ken Young,
'Perspectives on Policy Analysis'. Public Administration Bulletin,
No.25, December 1977, p.27.   Used with permission.

scepticism will ensue. Policy advocacy is scarcely a pioneering
breakthrough. In Britain, the work of the Webbs and the other
Fabians can be described as policy advocacy without any stretch of the
imagination. A similar point can also be made about the contributions
of various individuals, institutes and bureaux at the time of the
Depression, the New Deal and the Second World War in the United
States.(10) The antecedents of information for policy lie in the
decades before the publication of The Policy Sciences. Economists
have been involved in the evaluation of government policies for many
years - e.g. defence, water.(11) Studies of the policy-making
process is but another way of describing the community power
literature.(12) Output studies may be a current preoccupation but
work in this idiom began over 15 years ago.(13) The development of
techniques such as PPBS or Cost Benefit Analysis are scarcely of
recent origin. There is no paucity of work on particular policy
areas.(14) In fact, scepticism seems altogether too mild a reaction
to the claim of newness. It is all very familiar.

In pointing to the diversity and longevity of the interest in public
policy-making, there is the danger of belabouring the obvious. However, the exercise does serve to pose, again but in a more acute form,
the question of what is new about the current interest in public
policy-making. A third, and final, attack on this question can be
made by examining the origins of the current interest.

Two factors seem to be overwhelmingly important in the recent
development of the study of public policy-making in the United States.
First, the massive growth in the scope and extent of government intervention and, second, the provision of funds to universities for the
establishment of institutes devoted to this area of interest. This
is not to deny that, at least in part, the origins lie in academic
developments. It is to emphasise that without a 'market' for the
study of public policy-making, the development would, in all
probability, not have occurred on the same scale. Amongst the
academic influences can be numbered the reaction against current ways
of studying public bureaucracies - against the curricula of departments
of Public Administration with their focus on budgeting, personnel and
management. Also worthy of note is the example set by independent
research institutes such as Brookings and Rand.(15) The development
in analytical techniques and research methodologies in the post-war
period also made it more feasible (or at least plausible) that social
scientists had something to offer government. But of all these
academic influences, attention should perhaps be focused on the
search for 'relevance' on the part of the social sciences.

'Relevance' is, of course, more a rallying-cry than an analytical
category. It represents the dissatisfactions of social scientists
with their individual professions. It does not encompass such
emotive forms of involvement as the abortive 'Project Camelot', nor
does it refer to the 'New Mandarins'.(16) Rather, it reflects a
rejection of the sterility said to be associated with the 'behavioural
revolution', or at least its worst excesses. It is a form of
expiation for involvement in Vietnam - for 'the role that American
intellectuals have played in designing and implementing policy...';
for ' ... a younger intelligentsia, trained up in the pragmatic

dispensation, immensely ready for the executive ordering of events ...'(17). Also, it is a response to the 'Great Society' and the massive programmes for social renewal. Academic developments cannot be explained in isolation from the society within which the occur. The interest in public policy-making is as much a product of the stress and turmoil in American society as any of the specific policies of the period. But this amalgam of influences did not prompt only the interest in public policy-making. It also shaped the form of that interest. More specifically, the emphasis fell on Policy Analysis rather than on Policy Studies. And at this juncture it is possible to essay an answer at least to the question of what is distinctive about the current interest in the study of public policy-making. The answer is - Policy Analysis. And policy analysis has the following characteristics:

(a) Analytical

Policy analysis utilises the analytical techniques and research methodologies developed in the post-war period, particularly those developed in economics, and applies them to current government problems.

(b) Multi-disciplinary

Policy analysis draws upon any discipline for relevant information and expertise. In particular, political science and economics are, at worst, coexisting in the same building in an effort to undertake inter-disciplinary work rather than talk about it.

(c) Problem Oriented

Policy analysis does not aim to develop theory (pure research) but to provide solutions to the current problems of government (policy research).

(d) Client Centred

The selection and definition of the problems for study is a product of continuous dialogue between government actors and the policy analyst.

Longer lists of characteristics have been set out to describe policy analysis but the above four characteristics seem to be central.(18) And they betray the origins in an era of increasing government intervention and of the search for 'relevance' amongst social scientists.

It is not obvious that policy analysis thus characterised is an entirely new development. At most, it could be described as a renewal of interest in a subject matter which had for decades formed the core of Public Administration. In addition, as argued above, policy analysis can be sub-divided into a number of different activities. There is no one activity called policy analysis. Perhaps its most distinctive, if not new, feature is the scale of the enterprise. In a relatively short time, many university departments and institutes have emerged to promote the study, teaching and application of policy analysis. However, this kind of assessment is too modest -

certainly for the proponents of policy analysis. It is claimed that policy analysis brings together descriptive studies and analytical techniques to improve government policies and policy-making. And the distinctive nature of this integrative effort is constantly reiterated. There is a strangely familiar ring to the claim that policy analysis is a discipline; to the question of 'Do we have a distinctive methodology?'; and to the search for a 'paradigm'. For example, Quade simply assumes that policy analysis is a discipline.(19)   Wildavsky has attacked the search for 'Aristotelian essences' precisely because the search is undertaken.   There are a variety of disquisitions on the methodology of policy analysis.(20)

The development of policy analysis and the claim to disciplinary status cannot be divorced from academic politics.   'Public Administration bashing' was a popular blood sport amongst the advocates of policy analysis.(21)   It led to an exaggeration of the virtues of policy analysis and the claim to a distinctive methodology formed the basis for the new discipline to replace Public Adminis-tration.   It bolstered the case for funds and organisational recog-nition within the universities.   Policy analysis became the latest academic fashion.   But the claim of distinctiveness is not solely the product of political expediency and, in order to evaluate it, it is particularly relevant to examine both the role of the social scientist in policy-making and the various theories of policy-making/decision-making.

These two topics, or more accurately 'dilemmas', are central to the claimed distinctiveness of policy analysis.   If it does not integrate descriptions of the policy-making process (and their underlying theories) with analytical techniques, thereby enabling the social scientist to play an effective role in policy-making, then there is little which is distinctive, or even new about policy analysis.   In terms of the definition given earlier, policy analysis becomes economists and political scientists studying that subject matter termed Public Administration.

(ii)   THE ROLE OF THE SOCIAL SCIENTIST IN POLICY-MAKING

One of the more stringent critics of the ability of social scientists to play an effective role in policy-making is Daniel Moynihan.   His central tenet is that:

       ' ... social science is at its weakest, at its worst, when
       it offers theories of individual or collective behaviour
       which raise the possibility, by controlling certain inputs,
       of bringing mass behavioral change.'(22)

In other words, the social sciences have produced innumerable discrete propositions which vary in their validity and applicability with a consequent inability to make reliable predictions.   As a result, the social scientist should not claim the legitimacy of science to gain preferential access for policy proposals.   He has no predictive know-ledge to offer government.   He is, and ought to be, as any other citizen with policy preferences.   As a social scientist he should steer clear of policy formulation.   Rather, he should concentrate on the

evaluation of results.   Only the most cursory knowledge of the
American poverty programme - or Vietnam, if you prefer - should serve
to illustrate the limits of social science as a guide to policy
formulation.(23)

  This issue has to be raised, albeit briefly, because it highlights
one of the major schisms in policy analysis.   On the one hand, policy
analysis is concerned with the description and explanation of the
causes and consequences of government policy as, for example, in
evaluation studies.   On the other hand, policy analysis is concerned
with prescription - with instrumental knowledge which is action-
oriented, and with policy advocacy.(24)   As Moynihan has emphasised,
however, the ability of social scientists to design policies which can
solve social problems is limited because our understanding of these
problems is woefully inadequate.   There is an additional dimension to
the problem in policy analysis which arises from its tendency to
advocate the introduction of 'rational' decision-making - i.e. the
cyclical process of setting objectives, identifying and comparing
alternatives, feedback and review (see below).   It is argued that, if
the government decision-making process was more rational, then the
resultant policies in particular policy areas would be more effective.
In other words, policy analysis prescribes for the introduction of a
rational process of decision-making in the anticipation that such a
rational process will make governments better able to predict.   But
even when the aim is to introduce rational decision-making and not to
make substantive predictions in a particular policy area, there are
severe problems.   Descriptions of the policy process emphasise the
limits to rationality.   The attempts to increase the rational component
in decision-making have met with, at best, limited success. Accordingly,
some writers avoid prescription and focus on the unintended consequences
of government policy in an effort to find out what went wrong.   Yet
others, undaunted by the problems of prediction or the limits to
rationality, continue to prescribe for rational policy-making in
government.

  The discontinuity between description and prescription is very
marked.   Its origins lie in the different theories of decision-making
- of which more in a moment.   Its consequences can be seen in the
profusion and confusion of roles of the social scientist in policy-
making.

  Paralleling the three types of policy analysis identified above, it is
possible to identify at least three possible roles for social scientists
in policy-making - the social critic, the analyst and the technician.(25)
The social critic role is a time-honoured one in the social sciences.
It involves the critical scrutiny of government policy with a particular
emphasis on values.   This can be in terms of the values which a given
policy serves or an assessment of the merits of a policy against the
values held by the social scientist.   Invariably, the social scientist
advocates particular policies or reforms in the light of his analysis.
The technician, on the other hand, takes the values as given.   His
role is to evaluate the means selected for achieving a particular goal
and to measure as precisely as possible problems selected by government
actors.   As such, the role is very similar to that of the academic who
is not concerned to advise government.   The description and analysis

of the causes and consequences of a particular policy can dominate the
work of the technician.   Prescription can be a marginal component in
his work.   The policy analyst role attempts to straddle the ground in
between these two positions.   Although he will not directly confront
the values of government actors with his own values, he will critically
scrutinise those values.   He will evaluate policies and measure
problems, but in so doing he will also propose policy options.   The
distinctiveness of policy analysis lies in the analyst role which
attempts to combine both the concern with values and technical skills
and expertise.   Through such an integration,government policy and
policy-making can be improved.   Unfortunately, it is this very
integration which has proved so difficult to achieve.   In the words of
Alice Rivlin:

> 'If any analyst thought it was going to be easy to make
> social action programs work better or to make more rational
> choices among programs, he is by now a sadder and a wiser
> man.   The choices are genuinely hard and the problems are
> extraordinarily complex and difficult.'(26)

Echoing Moynihan, she goes on to suggest that the contribution of the
analyst lies in the measurement of problems and the evaluation of the
consequences of programmes.(27)   There has been a retreat from the
halcyon days when macro-reform schemes like PPBS promised a rational
future today.   And the retreat itself illustrates the problem
surrounding the role of the social scientist in policy-making.
Distinctiveness lies in the ability of policy analysis to foster
rational analysis and thence to identify solutions to problems - i.e.
in the ability to predict.   And yet it is at this very point that the
limits to rationality appear to be most intransigent.   As a result,
the distinctiveness of policy analysis becomes blurred.   It can
hardly be claimed that describing and critically evaluating government
policies is a new or distinctive activity for academics.   The growing
prominence of the technician role and of evaluation studies is a
testimony to the failure of policy analysis to define its distinctive
contribution.(28)

The retreat from macro-reform schemes and the increasingly modest
definitions of the role of the social scientist could both be interpreted
as the growth of realism: a greater appreciation of the complexity of
government decision-making.   It can be seen also as evidence of the
intransigent nature of the limits to rationality.   It is to an
examination of these limits that I now turn.

(iii)   THE THEORIES OF DECISION-MAKING

If policy analysis cannot define a clear role for the social scientist
in policy-making, nor can it point to an agreed theory of decision-
making.   There are a number of competing theories of decision-making
and their mutually exclusive nature further weakens the claim to
distinctiveness.

Three models of decision-making can be identified - the rational, the
organisational and the political models.(29)   In the first instance,

the three models are defined.

The Rational Model

(a) Establish a complete set of operational goals with weights.

(b) Establish a complete inventory of other values and resources with weights.

(c) Prepare a complete set of alternative policies.

(d) Prepare a complete set of predictions of the benefits and costs of each alternative.

(e) Calculate the net expectation for each alternative.

(f) Compare the net expectations and identify the alternative(s) with the highest net expectation.(30)

The Organisational Model

(a) Choice is exercised with respect to a limited, approximate simplified model of the real situation - administrative man is boundedly rational.

(b) The model of the situation is not given but is a product of the choosers' own activities and the activities of others in his environment.

(c) The model of the situation generates standards of choice which are satisfactory.

(d) An alternative is satisfactory where there exists a set of criteria that describe mimimally satisfactory alternatives and where the alternative in question meets or exceeds all these criteria.(31)

(e) Decisions are not directed towards a unitary goal. The organisation is composed of groups with conflicting goals.

(f) The process of bargaining and negotiation between these groups leads to the emergence of a dominant coalition with an agreed set of temporary goals.

(g) The process of bargaining and negotiation is continuous and conflict over goals is ever-present.(32)

The Political Model

(a) The selection of value goals and empirical analysis of the needed action are not distinct from one another but are closely intertwined.

(b) Since means and ends are not distinct, means-ends analysis is often inappropriate or limited.

(c) The test of a 'good' policy is typically that various analysts find themselves directly agreeing on a policy (without their agreeing that it is the most appropriate means to an agreed objective).

(d) Analysis is drastically limited. Important possible outcomes are neglected. Important alternative potential policies are neglected. Important affected values are neglected.

(e) A succession of comparisons greatly reduces or eliminates reliance on theory.(33)

The first point to be emphasised is simply that it is possible to identify three different models of decision-making. It is often assumed that the rational model is the dominant 'paradigm' for policy analysis. Although it would be foolish to deny its importance, nonetheless it would be equally unwise to disregard the alternative models. As I shall argue in Chapter 4, the different conceptions of the decision-making process lead to very different curricula. More significantly, to posit a dominant paradigm is to miss the key issue in policy analysis - namely, the absence of a common theory of decision-making and the subsequent 'identity crisis'.

Although each of the models highlights certain features of the decision-making process, none is without its defects. The criticisms of the rational model have been made so often and so cogently, that they will be listed only briefly here. They are as follows:
(a) the precise and explicit statement of values incurs high political costs and, as a result, is avoided by politicians, but operational goals cannot be derived without a clear statement of values;
(b) there is no known method of ordering and weighting values;
(c) it is not possible to list all alternatives;
(d) the information available to the policy-maker is both imperfect and limited;
(e) it is not possible to predict the consequences of alternatives and the more original the alternative, the less possible are predictions; and
(f) it is not possible to cost all alternatives because of weaknesses (a) to (e) and because of the arbitrary nature of the assumptions involved in costing (e.g. ascribing monetary values to intangibles).(34)

This list of defects is formidable and has led to revisions of the model. It is argued that the model should be applied only in so far as it is feasible to do so given the scarcity of information, resources, analysts and original alternatives. The resultant decision may not be 'optimal' or fully rational but it will be more rational than, or at least preferable to, current methods of making decisions. The claim has become one of some analysis leads to more rational decisions than no analysis.

A critical evaluation of the organisational model is complicated because there is no single statement of the model. There are a number of versions which differ in key respects. In Herbert Simon's version there is the problem that he does not explain how satisfactory standards are generated. It has been alleged that 'satisficing' is such a broad concept that it covers any and all decision rules except 'optimisation'.(35)   Although Simon claims to be providing a description of decision-making, he emphasises the search for alternatives, the distinctions between means/ends and fact/values and techniques for improving decision-making.   There is a prominent prescriptive component in the model - a conclusion supported by Simon's later work on aids to decision-making, especially the use of computers.(36)   Simon's model has its roots in a reaction against the rational model in its unmodified form, but it retains elements of that model and remains vulnerable to the same criticisms.

The development of the organisational model by Cyert and March attempts to overcome a number of these problems.   Their description of goal setting as a political process begins to suggest how satisfactory standards are generated - they are a product of the agreement negotiated between groups within the organisation.   Nonetheless, problems remain.   Cyert and March focus on top management.   They do not analyses the 'plurality of social systems' within the organisation and, in particular, they do not explore how lower order participants influence decisions.(37)   Nor does their account explain how the aspirations of the various groups are formed or how the distribution of power affects the relationships between groups.(38)   These problems are not necessarily insurmountable,(39) but, from the point of view of policy analysis, there is one overwhelming limitation to this model. Its prime aim is to describe the process of organisational decision-making.   As a result, it emphasises the constraints on rational decision-making.   It does not indicate how decision-making can be improved.

Professor Lindblom's political or incremental model of decision-making similarly emphasises the constraints on rational decision-making. The model rejects the procedural, economic definition of rationality typified by the rational model.   'Agreement' replaces 'cost-benefit ratios' as the criterion of a 'good' policy.   Political rationality is primary.   Paul Diesing has argued that:

'Political rationality is the fundamental kind of reason, because it deals with the preservation and improvement of decision structures, and decision structures are the sources of all decisions.   Unless a decision structure exists, no reasoning and no decisions are possible ... There can be no conflict between political rationality and ... technical, legal, social or economic rationality, because the solution of political problems makes possible an attack on any other problem,while a serious political deficiency can prevent or undo all other problem solving.'(40)

The incremental model exemplifies this view.

The rational model or 'rational-comprehensive' approach to decision-making is abandoned as impossible.   Instead Lindblom argues that decisions are made following a strategy of 'successive limited comparisons' or 'disjointed incrementalism' - that is, decision-makers proceed step-by-step and policies change only marginally.   In this process, each decision-maker or 'partisan' continually adjusts to the decisions and interests of other decision-makers.   The multiplicity of actors and decisions are coordinated through this process of 'partisan mutual adjustment'. Agreement on the goals or objectives of a policy may not be possible, but it is possible to agree on specific courses of action.

Clearly this approach has a number of similarities with the organisational model - i.e. the criticisms of the rational model and the emphasis on goal setting as a political or bargaining process. However, there are important differences of emphasis. Most importantly, the incremental model has its roots in pluralist theories of American society. Bargaining is not limited, therefore, to bureaucratic actors but includes pressure groups and political parties. This is a considerable increase in the range of actors seen to impinge on decision-making. The focus of the organisational model is the bureaucratic actor, whereas the political model includes any actor within the political system.

Although descriptively persuasive in many respects, there are problems with the incremental model. The definition of an incremental change appears to be subjective. One man's increment is another man's revolution. The term is used to describe both the difference between policy X and policy Y and the process of getting from X to Y. Nor is the analysis purely descriptive. In describing how policy is made, it prescribes how policy ought to be made. The descriptive elements of the model do not specify the conditions under which incremental change is applicable. If a problem intensifies rapidly, should the attendant changes be limited to the margin? If innovative alternatives are available, should they be ignored for marginal changes? Moreover, is it true that governments take no fundamental decisions? Is it not possible that a fundamental decision sets the context for innumerable incremental decisions and that incremental decisions open the way to fundamental shifts in policy by easing the transition?(41)

Nor are the problems limited to the descriptive aspects of the model. Prescriptively it fails to recognise the inequalities between competing groups in society and, as a result, appears to defend the present as the best of all possible worlds. By defending what is, it has the potential for discouraging innovation and encouraging inertia.(42)

It can be suggested, therefore, that each of the models is selective. As Allison has pointed out:

> 'These conceptual models are much more than simple angles of vision or approaches. Each conceptual framework consists of a cluster of assumptions and categories that influence what the analyst finds puzzling, how he formulates his question, where he looks for evidence, and what he produces as an answer'.(43)

Not only is each model selective, but there is a sharp contrast of aims between the rational model on the one hand and the organisational and political models on the other. Substantially, if not exclusively, the latter models can be viewed as statements of the limitations of the rational model. They point, in the case of the political model, to the difficulties created for the rational model by pluralistic bargaining where the need for agreement precludes the specification of objectives; and, in the case of the organisational model, to the difficulties created where bureaucratic actors are not the passive, neutral instruments of political leaders but political actors in their own right, seeking to attain their own objectives and/or defend their own departmental interests. The rational model can be seen, therefore, as a prescriptive statement as to how decisions ought to be taken whereas the other two models qualify the prescription by describing how decisions are actually taken.

Thus, there is no one model of decision-making; each model is selective; and the models are either prescriptive or descriptive, but none blends these two elements together.(44) As a result, it could be argued that policy analysis is not a discrete, identifiable approach to the study of government. The literature which describes and discusses these models is now vast. There is no need, however, to review it in its entirety. A reference to the debate surrounding PPBS will illus- trate some of the consequences that have followed in the wake of these different conceptions of governmental decision-making. At first glance it might appear that the debate over PPBS focused on the feasibility of its implementation. However, the different evaluations of this reform stem from more fundamental considerations. The clash is between those advocating the rational model and those espousing the political model. One side sees only the inadequacy of current methods of government decision-making and the need for more rational decisions. The other side describes why current decision-making is as it is, and sees only the difficulties of affecting any change. The models, like all models, simplify and select from the available information, only in this case what is selected is so vastly different that they appear to be exploring different worlds.(45) If policy analysis is distinctive, its distinctiveness does not lie in any common theoretical stance.

(iv)   CONCLUSIONS

Public administration is a diverse subject. At any given point in time a range of disciplines will be studying a multitude of topics. Those involved do not share a 'paradigm' only   an area of investigation. Policy analysis is one of the more recent arrivals on the scene and, like many new arrivals, it has made its presence felt if only by the inconvenience it has caused. As an intellectual challenge in the study of public bureaucracies, policy analysis is a welcome development. As a new discipline or 'paradigm' the most impressive aspect of policy analysis is the extent to which it contains the problems and paradoxes of yesterday. In part its origins lie in a critique of the discipline of Public Administration and like this rival policy analysis lacks intellectual coherence. It has focused attention on the study of public bureaucracies when, for much of the 1960s, this was a neglected area of academic inquiry. It has ensured that the quantitative approaches developed elsewhere in the social sciences have been applied to the study of public bureaucracies. Above all, it has been a stimulus to intellectual debate. But without a theory of decision- making which can provide the basis for the introduction of a rational process of policy-making, its ability to make predictions in substantive policy areas and to provide a clear definition of the role(s) of social scientists in policy-making is heavily circumscribed. It would be

better viewed as a label expressing the desire of social scientists to
be 'relevant'. This is not to deny that the social scientist or the
policy analyst can do useful work for the government. It is to argue
that such work should focus on the description and measurement of
problems and the evaluation of the consequences of policies. Above
all, it is to argue that this kind of work does not warrant claims of a
new discipline or of a distinctive new contribution from social
scientists. It is a plea for modesty in the face of the very real
difficulties of prediction in the social sciences. The desire to be
relevant boils down to the need for more social scientists with the
courage to tackle problems rather than debate methodologies. You can
call such research by any name you wish - policy analysis, policy
studies, public administration - but whatever the rose is called, it
will be the sheer quality of the research done which will determine
how sweet it smells to the policy-maker.(46)

   Public administration in America is a stimulating area of academic
endeavour. To the visiting British academic it is an enterprise of
unparalleled scope, vigour and size. The analysis of current developments by many American commentators seems to be reluctant to recognise
this state of affairs. Myopia seems to be the order of the day.
Vigour is mistaken for confusion and eclecticism for disarray. The
desire and search for integration will continue, of course, but it must
not result in a loss of perspective. Diversity should be seen for the
source of strength that it is: for the debate and ferment that it
generates. Instead of bemoaning the lack of a discipline or a
'paradigm', the range of studies from a variety of disciplines could be
appreciated for the intellectual depth they provide in understanding a
highly complex subject. In a review of the future of Public Administration Dwight Waldo reflects, rather sadly, that:

   "If Public Administration should disappear in a restructuring
   and renaming of the disciplinary-educational-professional
   universe, the disappearance would be for many a cause of
   regret. But if this occurs it will be essentially incidental:
   Public Administration will have served its historical purpose
   of bridge and matrix and be more or less incorporated into a
   new pattern or synthesis.'(47)

   It is perhaps a little premature to signal the demise of the
discipline of Public Administration, but Waldo is indubitably correct
in his claim that the subject matter will survive albeit in a different
guise. It has never been successfully confined within the bounds of
a single discipline. Policy analysis has not, as yet, restructured
the disciplinary universe. If 'Public Administration is policy-
making', then policy analysis is also Public Administration. It faces
the same problem of heterogeneity. 'Intellectual crisis' and the
'paradigm problem' are common to both.

NOTES AND REFERENCES

(1)   H.D. Lasswell, "The Policy Orientation' in D.Lerner and H.D.
   Lasswell (eds.), The Policy Sciences, Stanford University Press,
   Stanford, California, 1951, pp.3-15.

(2)   D.Waldo, 'Organisation Theory: an elephantine problem', Public Administration Review (21) 1961: pp.210-25.

(3)   The argument in this chapter incorporates material previously published in R.A.W.Rhodes,'A Rose by Any Other Name: five books in search of policy analysis', Local Government Studies (3) No.3, 1977: pp.71-83.   I would like to thank Charles Knight & Co. and the editor of Local Government Studies for permission to use this material.

(4)   E.S.Quade, Analysis for Public Decision, American Elsevier, New York, 1975, p.4.

(5)   T.R. Dye, Understanding Public Policy, Prentice Hall, Englewood Cliffs, N.J., 1972, p.3.   Other examples of the same approach include R.I.Hofferbert, The Study of Public Policy, Bobbs-Merrill, New York, 1974; and C.O.Jones, An Introduction to the Study of Public Policy, Wadsworth, Belmont, California, 1970.

(6)   H.D.Lasswell, A Pre-view of Policy Sciences, American Elsevier, New York, 1971, p.1.

(7)   Quoted in R.F.Ericson, 'The Policy Analysis Role of the Contemporary University', Policy Sciences (1) 1970: pp.429-42

(8)   A.Wildavsky, 'Principles for a Graduate School of Public Policy', Public Administration Bulletin, No.26, April 1978, p.12 and p.17.

(9)   See , for example, the definition and discussion in Y.Dror, Public Policymaking Reexamined, Chandler, Scranton, Penn., 1968, pp.241-44.

(10)   For a description of the policy role of social scientists in the 1930s and 1940s see R.Egger, 'The Period of Crisis: 1933 to 1945', in F.C.Mosher (ed.), American Public Administration: Past. Present, Future, University of Alabama Press, Alabama, 1975, pp.49-96.

(11)   See, for example, C.Hitch and R.McKean, The Economics of Defence in the Nuclear Age, Harvard University Press, Cambridge, Mass., 1960; and A.Maass et al., Design of Water Resource Systems, Harvard University Press, Cambridge, Mass., 1962.

(12)   See, for example, R.A.Dahl, Who Governs? Yale University Press, New Haven, 1961.

(13)   See, for example, R.E.Dawson and J.A.Robinson, 'Inter-party Competition, Economic Variables and Welfare Policies in the States', Journal of Politics (25) 1963: pp.265-89.

(14)   A select bibliography of studies of particular policy areas can be found in G.E.Caiden, The Dynamics of Public Administration: guidelines to current transformations in theory and practice, Dryden Press, Hinsdale, Illinois, 1971, pp.315-16.

(15)   The variety of research institutes is mapped, albeit provisionally, in I.L.Horowitz and J.E.Katz, Social Science and Public Policy in the United States, Praeger, New York, 1975.   See also B.L.R.Smith, The RAND Corporation: case study of a non-profit advisory corporation, Harvard University Press, Cambridge, Mass., 1966.

(16)   On 'Project Camelot' see I.L.Horowitz (ed.), The Rise and Fall of Project Camelot, MIT Press, Cambridge, Mass., 1967.

(17)   N.Chomsky, American Power and the New Mandarins, Penguin Books, Harmondsworth, 1969, pp.9-10.

(18)   See, for example, Dror, Public Policymaking Reexamined, pp.241-44. For a similar characterisation see, amongst others, N.Beckman, 'Introduction', Public Administration Review (37) No.3., 1977: pp.221-22.

(19)   Quade, Analysis for Public Decisions, p.10.

(20)   See, for example, J.S.Coleman, Policy Research in the Social

<u>Sciences</u>, General Learning Corporation, Morristown, N.J., 1972.

(21)   For example, Harry Weiner describes Public Administration as
'venerable' and 'second-rate'.   He also adds: 'Where once a
distinguishing characteristic of the public administration student
was that he could not financially afford law school, or had not the
grades to be admitted, or neither, the student on policy analysis
programs had to be a top student'.   H. Weiner, 'A New Education For
Public Service?' <u>Urban Analysis</u> (3) 1976: pp.83-87.   In a similar
vein, Jack Walker suggests that public administration programmes
' ... lagged behind the latest developments in social research,
management science and economic analysis'; and that social and
political developments in American society 'did not provoke a
vigorous response from established graduate programs in public
administration'.   Policy analysis is the response to the 'growing
intellectual irrelevance of traditional courses in public administration'.   J.L.Walker, 'The Curriculum in Public Policy Studies at
the University of Michigan', <u>Urban Analysis</u> (3) 1976: pp.89-103.

(22)   D. Moynihan, <u>Maximum Feasible Misunderstanding</u>, The Free Press,
New York, 1969, p.191.

(23)   For more general discussions of the limits to expert advice see
H.Wilensky, <u>Organisational Intelligence</u>, Basic Books, New York, 1967;
A.B.Cherns, R.Sinclair and W.I.Jenkins (eds.), <u>Social Science and
Government: Policies and Problems</u>, Tavistock, London, 1972; and L.J.
Sharpe, 'Social Scientists and Policymaking: some cautionary thoughts
and transatlantic reflections', <u>Policy and Politics</u> (4) No.2., 1975:
pp.7-34.

(24)   This schism is illustrated by the exchange between Professors
Dror and Dye in the <u>Policy Studies Journal</u>.   See Y.Dror, 'General
Policy Science', <u>Policy Studies Journal</u> (1) No.1, 1972: pp.4-6 and 47;
T.R. Dye, 'Policy Analysis and Political Science; some problems at
the interface', <u>Policy Studies Journal</u> (1) No.2, 1972: pp.103-107; and
Y.Dror, 'Some Diverse Approaches to Policy Analysis: a partial reply
to Thomas Dye', <u>Policy Studies Journal</u> (1) No.4, 1972: pp.258-60.
See also T.R. Dye, <u>Policy Analysis,</u> University of Alabama Press,
Alabama, 1976.

(25)   For a detailed discussion of the various role orientations of
policy analysts in public bureaucracies, as distinct from social
scientists who may or may not be in government employment, see
A.Meltsner, <u>Policy Analysis in the Bureaucracy,</u> University of
California Press, Berkeley, 1976.

(26)   A.Rivlin, <u>Systematic Thinking for Social Action</u>, The Brookings
Institution, Washington D.C., 1971, p.5.

(27)   For a discussion of evaluation, and a useful bibliography, see
C.H.Weiss, <u>Evaluation Research:methods of assessing program effectiveness,</u> Prentice Hall, Englewood Cliffs N.J., 1972.

(28)   This failure is illustrated also by the absence of any
distinctive policy analysis literature.   Rather, there are a range
of studies from a variety of disciplines.   See, for example, the
studies cited in Professor Dror's bibliographic essay in Dror, <u>Public
Policymaking Reexamined</u>, pp.327-56.

(29)   For a similar but not identical approach to the various models
of decision-making see G.Allison, <u>Essence of Decision</u>, Little, Brown,
Boston, 1971.

(30)   For a full statement of this model see Dror, <u>Public Policymaking
Reexamined</u>, pp.134 ff.

(31)   For a full statement see H.A.Simon, <u>Administrative Behaviour,</u>

The Free Press, New York, second edition, 1957.
(32)   For a full statement see R.M.Cyert and J.G.March, A Behavioural
Theory of the Firm, Prentice Hall, Englewood Cliffs, N.J., 1963.
(33)   For a full statement see C.I.Lindblom, 'The Science of Muddling
Through', Public Administration Review (19) 1959: pp.79-88; and
C.I.Lindblom, The Intelligence of Democracy, The Free Press, New
York, 1965.
(34)   These points are summarised from Dror, Public Policymaking
Reexamined, pp.133-41.   See also H.R. van Gunsteren, The Quest for
Control, Wiley, New York, 1976.
(35)   See L.C. Gawthrop, Bureaucratic Behaviour in the Executive Branch,
The Free Press, New York, 1969, pp.90-91.
(36)   See, for example, H.A.Simon, The New Science of Management
Decision, Harper and Row, New York, 1960.
(37)   T. Burns, 'On the Plurality of Social Systems', in T.Burns (ed.),
Industrial Man, Penguin Books, Harmondsworth, 1969, pp.232-49.
(38)   A.M.Pettigrew, The Politics of Organisational Decision-making,
Tavistock, London, 1973, pp.9-10.
(39)   See, for example, Pettigrew, The Politics of Organisational
Decision-making; and M.Crozier, The Bureaucratic Phenomenon, Chicago
University Press, Chicago, 1964.
(40)   P.Diesing, Reason in Society, University of Illinois Press,
Urbana, 1962, pp.198 and 203-204.
(41)   This point is taken from A.Etzioni, 'Mixed Scanning: a third
approach to decision-making', Public Administration Review (27) 1967:
pp.385-92.
(42)   For a discussion of these various criticisms see Y.Dror,
'Muddling Through - Science or Inertia?', Public Administration Review
(24) 1964: pp.153-7; and C.I.Lindblom, 'Contexts for Change and
Strategy: a reply', Public Administration Review (24) 1964: pp.157-8.
(43)   Allison, Essence of Decision, p.245.
(44)   For further evidence on the variety of approaches to policy
analysis see A.Etzioni, Social Problems, Prentice Hall, Englewood
Cliffs, N.J., 1976, pp.3-27.   Etzioni's attempt to blend together
the various approaches is fully argued in A.Etzioni, The Active
Society, The Free Press, New York, 1968.
(45)   For example compare D.Novick, Program Budgeting, Harvard
University Press, Cambridge, Mass., 1965, with A.Wildavsky, 'The
Political Economy of Efficiency: cost-benefit analysis, systems
analysis and program budgeting', Public Administration Review (26)
1966: pp.292-310, with M.J. White, 'The Impact of Management Science
on Political Decision Making,' in F.J.Lyden and E.G.Miller (eds.)
Planning Programming Budgeting: a systems approach to management,
Markham, Chicago, second edition 1972, pp.395-423.
(46)   This discussion of policy analysis has focused on its weaknesses.
To end on a more positive note, the ways in which policy studies could
develop are discussed in R.Simeon, 'Studying Public Policy', Canadian
Journal of Political Science (IX) No.4, 1976: pp.548-80.
(47)   D.Waldo, 'Education for Public Administration in the Seventies',
in F.C.Mosher (ed.), American Public Administration: Past, Present,
Future, University of Alabama Press, Alabama, 1975, p.226.

4 Teaching Public Administration and Policy Analysis in America

(i)   INTRODUCTION

A distinction has been drawn between the subject matter of Public
Administration and the institutional form through which that subject
matter is taught.   It has been suggested that the subject matter is
too eclectic to be confined to a single discipline called 'Public
Administration'.   Accordingly, the teaching of Public Administration
is not limited to university departments bearing that name.   Public
Administration is taught through a variety of institutional forms.   In
the previous chapters, I have concentrated on mapping the diverse
approaches to the subject matter.   In this chapter, I turn away from
the broad context and focus on the institutions through which Public
Administration is taught.   In the first instance, the variety of
institutions is described.   Against this backcloth, I then examine in
some detail four taught masters' degrees - at Syracuse, Michigan,
Berkeley and Stanford.   In each case, I describe the programme as it
existed in the academic year 1975-76.

   This analysis is based on the arguments developed in earlier chapters.
Because Public Administration is such a complex subject to which so
many disciplines contribute, each university or institute has to
specify its particular approach to teaching the subject.   More
specifically, a distinction can be drawn between the inclusive approach
which attempts to encompass all relevant disciplines in a teaching
programme and a focused approach, which selects between disciplines and
topics to produce a distinctive, discriminating programme.   I argue
that the focused approach is the appropriate response to the complexity
of Public Administration.

(ii)   THE INSTITUTIONAL BACKCLOTH

In 1973 the National Association of Schools of Public Affairs and
Administration sent a questionnaire to its member institutions seeking
information of the characteristics of their graduate programmes in
Public Administration.(1)   This survey provides a great deal of
information on the institutional forms through which Public Administration is taught and studied.   The survey demonstrates that there is
a variety of institutional structures.   Of the 101 institutions
replying to the questionnaire, 25 of the graduate programmes were
offered by a separate professional school of public affairs and
administration (PA/A).   A further 23 were offered by a separate
department of PA/A in a larger unit such as a social science division.
11 programmes were offered by a professional school of PA/A combined
with another professional school such as a business school.   6 were
offered by a department of PA/A combined with another department such
as business administration.   Finally, 36 programmes were offered as a
PA/A programme within a political science department.

   Thus, although political science remained an important home for
Public Administration, it was more common for it to be separated from

the discipline. Almost half the institutions replying to the questionnaire were independent and only 17 were part of a generic school of administration.(2)   It is commonly argued that a separate structure is essential for the development of Public Administration. Mackleprang and Fritschler comment, however, that the NASPAA data, at least at the aggregate level, show little systematic differences between separate and other institutional forms in their programme characteristics.   This conclusion applies to total number of faculty, number of areas of specialisation and number and type of degree requirements.(3)   At this juncture, the issues of the variety of forms and the relationship of form and development are simply raised.   I will discuss then in more detail when looking at the individual institutions.

The next point to be raised concerns the disciplinary nature of the various institutions.   To what extent is the description inter-disciplinary or multi-disciplinary an ideal or a reality when applied to Public Administration?   Two ways of assessing at least partially the multi-disciplinary nature of Public Administration are the range of specialist subjects offered to students and the range of specialisms of members of staff.   The NASPAA survey reports that 20 institutions offered 11 or more areas of specialisation and 32 institutions offered 6 to 10 areas of specialisation.   Moreover, two-thirds of respondents reported that their faculty covered more than 5 academic fields.   The specialisms most commonly represented were:

SPECIALISMS	NUMBER OF PROGRAMMES
Political Science	86
Public Administration	80
Economics	68
Business Administration	56
Sociology	51
Statistics-Mathematics	40
Law	38
Planning	37
Psychology	32

Many of these specialisms were represented on the important, policy-making committees of the schools.   This could be interpreted as indicating a high degree of commitment to multi-disciplinary work. Mackleprang and Fritschler suggest, however, that some care should be exercised in interpreting the figures.   The extent of multi-disciplinary work is more limited than the figures suggest.   For example, 65 per cent of 'other' faculty - i.e. not political science or public administration - were concentrated in 20 institutions.   In addition, these 20 institutions accounted for one-third of the political science/Public Administration faculty.   Multi-disciplinary work is, it would appear, the prerogative of the few.   Whether these figures mean that the subject as taught is not multi-disciplinary is unclear.   The multi-disciplinary nature of Public Administration lies in the variation in specialisms between institutions rather than in the variety within them.   No data is presented on this point - reflecting no doubt NASPAA's desire to encourage each institution to cover all the relevant specialisms.

NASPAA has produced guidelines and standards for higher degrees in Pub-ic Administration.(4)   They identify five subject matter areas - political, social and economic context; analytical tools; individual, group, organisational dynamics; policy analysis; and administrative/ management processes.   The schools did not offer courses across this range and, as the following list indicates, there appeared to be a continuing concentration on the staff functions of personnel, budgeting and organisational analysis and a corresponding weakness in analytical and quantitative tools:

COURSES	NUMBER OF PROGRAMMES
Organisation Theory and Behaviour	96
Public Policy	95
Public Finance	92
Urban Administration and Inter-Governmental Relations	92
Personnel	89
Planning	83
Administrative Law	79
Comparative Bureaucracy	74
International Administration	38
Analytical Methods	21

The conclusion which emerges from this brief survey is that:

' ... only about 40 of the programs have sufficient resources and balance to offer broad-based professional degrees in public affairs/public administration.   To varying degrees, the remaining programs lack the resources to provide an integrated, balanced graduate education in public affairs/public administration.'(5)

The institutions described below were indisputably in the 'Top Forty' and, accordingly, it should be remembered that any critical comments made probably applied with even greater force to the majority of schools of Public Administration.   It would appear, however, that, at least for a minority of institutions, Public Administration was a separate, multi-disciplinary activity teaching a wide variety of courses and employing a range of academic specialists.   That all did not conform to this picture is probably less surprising than the fact that a large number did, especially as 'there is every indication that a significant movement towards these objectives is under way'.(6)

The NASPAA survey of graduate programmes in Public Administration included the new policy studies and policy analysis programmes. However, given the prominence of such programmes in the recent history of Public Administration, they will be discussed separately and in a little more detail.   The first point to be made is that policy studies was widely taught and it was not limited to a few specialist institutions.   95 institutions offered an average of 3.5 courses per programme in the public policy field.   But the development of this area has become closely linked in many people's minds with the funding of policy analysis programmes by the Ford Foundation.   Since 1973, the Ford Foundation has supported the development of policy analysis programmes at 8 institutions - the Graduate School of Public Policy at Berkeley,

the School of Urban and Public Affairs at Carnegie-Mellon, the John F.
Kennedy School of Government at Harvard, the Institute of Public Policy
Studies at Michigan, the Graduate School of Business at Stanford, the
Lyndon B.Johnson School of Public Affairs at Texas, the Institute of
Policy Sciences and Public Affairs at Duke, and the Graduate Institute
of the Rand Corporation.(7)   This does not exhaust the list of
specialist degrees.   By 1976, public policy programmes had also been
established at Buffalo, Chicago, Claremont, Maryland, Minnesota, North
Carolina,Pennsylvania, Stony Brook and Yale.   Doubtless more have
emerged in recent years.   However, I concentrate on the programmes
supported by the Ford Foundation below.   These programmes share a
number of characteristics:

(a) The new programmes were set up as separate departments, institutes
    or schools.
(b) All emphasised the contribution of analytical techniques (e.g. cost-
    benefit analysis, micro-economics, statistics) to the study of public
    policy.
(c) The programmes were multi-disciplinary and offered a core
    curriculum commonly comprising economics, political science and
    quantitative techniques.
(d) Most programmes had a substantial 'experiential' component.
    Students were sent on placements ('internships') and, in addition,
    many of the individual courses stress the use of case material and
    working on 'real' problems.
(e) With the exception of Rand, all the new schools offered a master's
    degree.   For the most part this degree was seen as training for
    public service rather than an academic career.(8)

As one might expect from the discussion in Chapter 3, these
characteristics are seen as highly distinctive.   Thus Yates comments:

    ' ... the new programs represented a major departure from
    both traditional schools of public administration (which
    typically emphasised subjects like personnel administration
    and budgeting procedures) and schools of substantive policy
    (such as criminology, education, health).'(9)

However, this discussion of the common features should not be allowed
to obscure the very real differences between the various schools.
These differences will be explored in the case studies of particular
programmes.(10)

(iii)   THE INDIVIDUAL SCHOOLS

(a)   Department of Public Administration, Maxwell School of Citizen-
    ship and Public Affairs, Syracuse University

Founded in 1924, Syracuse provides one of the oldest university
programmes of academic training for the public service in the United
States.(11)   Throughout its long history the Maxwell School has been
involved in the development of Public Administration.   Dean W.E.
Mosher helped found the American Society of Public Administration.
The Public Administration Review was founded at Maxwell in 1937 and it

was edited at the School for many years.   Maxwell School is, therefore, one of the more prestigious homes of Public Administration.

In 1975/76 graduate teaching took a variety of forms.(12)   There was
a Masters of Public Administration (MPA) which was offered in two forms
and a Doctor of Philosophy in Public Administration (Ph.D.).
Programme I of the MPA consisted of a series of courses taught 'end-on-
end' - that is, each course was completed in three or four weeks of
intensive work, at which point the student began another course.   In
effect, each student had to take serially   12 compulsory or core
courses and   2 optional or elective courses.   Additional electives
could be substituted for core courses depending on the academic background of the student.   Clearly this   is a highly structured and
intensive degree as can be seen from the following schedule of courses
and their timing.

The Schedule of Programme I Courses at Syracuse University (1975/6)

Course Description	Dates
Summer	
Introduction to Public Administration	July 8 - July 18
Public Budgeting	July 21 - Aug. 29
The Administrator in the Political Environment	July 21 - Aug. 8
Fall	
Organisation Theory	Nov. 10 - Nov. 25
Organisation Development	Sept. 8 - Sept. 26
Introduction to Government Statistics	Sept. 29 - Oct. 17
Public Management	Oct. 20 - Nov. 7
Elective	Sept. 8 - Dec. 10
Spring	
Political Economy	Jan. 19 - Feb. 6
Personnel and Collective Bargaining	Feb. 16 - March 5
Quantitative Aids to Administration	March 15 - April 2
Ethics and Morality in Public Affairs	April 5 - April 23
Elective	Jan. 19 - April 23
Policy Analysis in Public Policymaking	May 4 - May 25

Course titles can be less than enlightening as to course content.
Brief descriptions of the above courses, and the core courses at all the
universities I visited, can be found in Appendix A.   Originally, the
programme was aimed at prospective city managers, but the original aims
have broadened considerably to encompass local, state and federal
employment.   Although Programme I was taken by students with a very
limited background in Public Administration, it was also taken by the
better qualified students who were not sure of their area of
specialisation or who wished to pursue a general course of study in
Public Administration.

Programme II was a more flexible version of the MPA which was formally begun in 1969. Although students had to take some intensive modules at the beginning and end of the year and some core courses, Programme II followed the normal semester format. Students had to demonstrate that they had a sound academic background in Public Administration - that is, in the core subjects contained in Programme I - but, subject to this requirement, they could specialise in a range of subjects. Apart from a traditional disciplinary focus, the available specialisms included metropolitan studies and health service delivery. Approximately 80 per cent of the 120 students were enrolled in Programme II, although the balance between core subjects and electives varied widely between individuals.

The Ph.D. programme was a combination of course work and dissertation. Broadly speaking, students devoted two-thirds of their time to course work and one-third to the dissertation. Of the course work, 60 per cent was devoted to the MPA or its equivalent, 10 per cent on an area of specialisation, 10 per cent on methodology and the remainder of the time to a number of required topics - e.g. scope and profession of Public Administration. The dissertation normally fell within the student's area of specialisation. There were approximately 25 students registered for the Ph.D.

Originally, the MPA and Ph.D. were offered as inter-disciplinary programmes drawn from the various department based disciplines available in the School. Since 1974, however, a separate Department of Public Administration within the School has had the primary responsibility for the programmes. It was still able, of course, to draw on faculty from the rest of the School and it did so extensively for many of its Programme II specialisms - e.g. metropolitan studies, health service delivery. In assessing the inter-disciplinary nature of Public Administration at Syracuse, however, the analysis is limited to members of the Department.

The majority of the Department avowed Political Science and/or Public Administration as their specialisation. Out of 23 tenured and visiting faculty, five were economists, two were lawyers and one a statistician.

The remaining 15 had a variety of special fields including education, administrative theory, metropolitan studies, public finance and personnel management, although described as Political Science and/or Public Administration specialists.

Turning next to the courses available in the Department, it can be seen from the following list that a wide variety were offered:

Courses Available at Syracuse University (1975/6): organised by the 5 NASPAA categories

A.   Political, Social, Economic and Intellectual Context

     (i) Core Subjects

          1. Organisation Theory or
             Ethics and Morality in Public Affairs or
             Ethics of Medicine and Biomedical Research

45

2. The Administrator in the Political Environment or
   Political Economy or
   Economic Processes or
   Macro-Micro Economics or
   Health Economics

(ii) Specialised Subjects

1. Public Administration and Democracy
2. Local Government Administration
3. Inter-governmental Social Services Delivery Systems
4. History of Public Administration: Washington to Ford
5. Comparative Administration
6. Management and Development
7. Washington Seminar
8. Advanced Public Administration

B. Analytical Tools

(i) Core Subjects

1. Introduction to Statistics in Government or
   Introduction to Statistical Estimation

2. Methods, Analysis and Evaluation or
   Quantitative Aids to Administration

(ii) Specialised Subjects

1. Information Sources and Programme Analysis
2. Econometrics I
3. Mathematics for Economists

C. Individual, Group and Organisation Behaviour

(i) Core Subjects

1. Organisational Development or
   Organisation Behaviour or
   Personnel and Organisation Development

(ii) Specialised Subjects

1. Techniques and Systems of Personnel Assessment

D. Policy Analysis

(i) Core Subjects

1. Policy Analysis in Public Policymaking or
   Policy Issues in Health Care Delivery Systems

(ii) Specialised Subjects

1. National Urban Policy Development
2. Social Policy Planning

        3. Introduction to Metropolitan Studies
        4. Public Policy in Higher/Post Secondary Education

E.   Administration and Management Processes

    (i)   Core Subjects

        1. Personnel and Collective Bargaining or
           Public Personnel Management

        2. Public Budgeting

        3. Public Management or
           Organisation and Management or
           Programme Management and Evaluation or
           Health Administration

    (ii)   Specialised Subjects

        1. Public Management of Technology
        2. Analysis of Local Public Services Delivery
        3. Administrative Law

    This is not a complete list of the courses taken by the Department's
students nor does the list signify that all the courses were taught by
members of the Department.   It does indicate the range of courses that
were available.

    From this picture of the Department, it should be clear that the
objective was to provide a broad range of courses (following the NASPAA
guidelines) suitable for educating future public employees.   As such,
the Department probably embodied the aspirations of many small Public
Administration Departments.   During my travels a number of people
expressed surprise at my visiting Syracuse.   When I explained that I
wanted to visit a traditional department of Public Administration eye-
brows were raised.   This poor image of traditional Public Administration
- a term I take to refer to any programme which includes such topics
as personnel and budgeting - was widespread and, as far as Syracuse was
was concerned, grossly unfair.   Everyone is allowed to find certain
subjects boring - I have some difficulty working up any enthusiasm for
personnel management - but the subject is not on that count rendered
irrelevant and unnecessary.   The NASPAA guidelines represent an attempt
to identify, with the advice of practitioners, the areas in which a
public manager needs educating.   It is argued that a new employee with
this range of knowledge is better prepared for public service than one
without it.   Programme I of the MPA did not claim to be a substitute
for on-the-job training nor did it claim to be preparing specialists
for a whole range of government functions.   In fact, students wishing
to specialise could and did take Programme II.   However, a prime
objective in the MPA was to imbue a range of knowledge and skills(13)
relevant to the prospective employees.   This inclusive approach is one
of a number of possible approaches to education for public sector
management.   Too often, especially in recent years, critics have
dismissed this approach out of hand.   It deserves a far more thorough
examination.   It is not my brief or desire to produce a defense of

inclusive approaches in Public Administration. I have attempted,
however, to state the case for the approach. I now propose to review
the Syracuse programme in some detail, and the obvious starting point
is the adequacy of the NASPAA guidelines. Some faculty at Syracuse
played a prominent role in the development of the guidelines which have
been accepted at Syracuse. They were designed explicitly 'to enhance
the quality of existing programs in public affairs/public administration'
and to 'provide criteria for evaluating the various facets of a program
and for denoting ways for improving the educational process and
student product.'(14) They are basic to the inclusive approach to
Public Administration and the following discussion of their adequacy
is central both to an evaluation of Syracuse's programmes and to an
assessment of teaching trends in American Public Administration.

   The NASPAA guidelines suggest that a public manager's professional
competence rests upon four basic elements: (1)knowledge; (2)skills;
(3)values; and (4) behaviour. As noted already, they also identify
five subject matter areas. Each element is related to each subject
matter area to produce a matrix containing twenty topic areas, although
it is not suggested that each topic should be a separate course. In
other words, the guidelines were an elaborate exercise. The problem
is their generality and the consequent difficulty of translating the
various topics into practice. For example, it is suggested that the
contextual subjects should teach: 'Tolerance of diverse views of other
persons and groups' and the 'Capacity to adjust to complex political-
social environments and situations.' Just how one is expected to
produce such tolerant, adaptive behaviour is unclear. ˊThe phrase
ignores also the question of tolerance for whom - the Weathermen?
Moreover, the sheer range of knowledge and skills suggested is so great
that some selection of content will have to take place. For example,
the topics included under analytical tools are sufficient to constitute
a master's degree in that subject alone, ranging as they do from
parametric and non-parametric statistics through computer use and
electronic data processing to socio-metric surveys and value analysis.
But no criteria are provided for deciding either the balance of topics
or the selection of some topics to the exclusion of others within a
subject matter area. Nor is it clear what balance should be struck
between subject matter areas. Finally, the designated subject matter
areas are so general that most universities would have some difficulty
using them to evaluate their curricula. If, for example, a university
offers already specialist courses in budgeting and personnel but not in
planning, management science, organisational development and programme
evaluation, does this mean its treatment of the subject matter area,
management/administrative processes, is inadequate? Should it offer a
general course covering all aspects in addition to its specialist
courses, or should each topic be a specialist course? NASPAA provides
no answers to these questions.

   Such a conclusion should surprise no one familiar with business schools or
the question 'What is a manager?' The problem of defining a manager's
role is perennial and central to the inclusive approach to public
sector management.(15) Unless the role can be defined, the knowledge
inputs necessary to train the future incumbent of that role must
remain either a product of 'guestimates' or at such a high level of
generality as to encompass every possible item of potentially relevant

knowledge. The NASPAA guidelines have no explicit definition of a manager's role and, accordingly, tend towards an all-encompassing generality. Each individual school must define, therefore, its own philosophy of management, its own view of the manager's role - a conclusion which brings the discussion back to Syracuse and its interpretation/application of the guidelines. Given that Syracuse has explicitly accepted these guidelines, to what extent are the confusion and ambiguities of the guidelines repeated in their teaching programmes?

Programme I of the MPA is essentially all-embracing. To eyes accustomed to British universities and their curricula, the students know a little bit about a lot of subjects but not very much about each one. It is a tough package. It is essentially introductory and, to this observer, it seemed to serve its purpose of providing a general preparation for public service. I remain unconvinced, however, that this approach is right. Because of the absence of a clear role definition, too much gound is covered to ensure that all conceivably relevant topics are included. As a result, students have only a cursory familiarity with many areas which, if any one proved important in their subsequent careers, they would have to begin learning virtually from scratch.

It has been strongly argued in rebuttal that only a minority of students took Programme I and that, under Programme II, students specialised in that area of greatest relevance to their future careers. The reply is at one and the same time accurate and misleading. Programme II did offer a number of specialisms but only some of these were available in the Department. Thus, an important issue arose over the prerequisites for taking a specialism. For example, metropolitan studies had a large economics input, the economics core course on the MPA was felt to be inadequate preparation for this specialism, and, unless the student had previous economics training, he was substantially handicapped if not disqualified from taking this set of electives. The same was true for the health service delivery specialism. As a result, only some 34 per cent of all MPA atudents specialised in the two major areas of metropolitan and health studies. Alternatively, for a number of other specialisms, the student carried a shopping bag around the university gathering together a package of courses as best he could. The Department was aware of this problem. Model curricula were produced to help the student. But even so, problems of conflicting timetables plagued the student taking courses in a number of departments. Moreover, the requirement that all students had to attend certain common modules and that electives could only be substituted when the core course requirements had been met, limited the degree of specialisation for what could appear to be an inflexible insistence on a comprehensive background knowledge.

It is not unfair to conclude, therefore, that Syracuse had a number of problems balancing the inclusive and focused approaches. On the one hand, the attempt was being made to meet the NASPAA standards with the result that Programme I contained a little bit about everything. On the other hand, specialist components were available in Programme II but the Department had a limited capacity to offer its own specialisms and students faced a series of constraints - some emanating from the core course requirements of the Department - in their attempts to specialise.

This conflict seemed to have at least some of its roots in the desire for departmental status for Public Administration. Originally the MPA and Ph.D. were programmes offered by several departments. The degrees were not enshrined in a department. In recent years, however, departmentalism had become stronger. This comment does not refer solely to the creation of the Department of Public Administration. The attitude of the other departments seemed to have an insular component - witness the debate over prerequisites for the various specialisms. As a result, the inter-disciplinary base to the degree was weaker than might appear to be the case on paper and the current trend appeared to be to weaken it further. The Department of Public Administration could be forced, not entirely against its will, into a situation of employing its own specialist and offering courses wholly from its own resources.

The effects of this growing departmentalism within the Maxwell School on the Department of Public Administration were marked. It created pressures on the Department to demonstrate its distinctiveness. Accordingly, there was a tendency to favour NASPAA's inclusive approach and an aspiration to teach the master's programme from its own resources. But this required additional financial and manpower resources which were less than readily available. Alternatively, the Department could demonstrate its distinctiveness by developing specialisms. But to do this, it encroached on the preserves of other departments. Herein lay the dilemma at Syracuse. Distinctiveness lay in either a self-contained Department of Public Administration or in the development of specialisms through inter-departmental work. Both avenues of progress were constrained, in the one case by lack of resources and in the other by 'departmentalism'.

To compound the problem, the type of specialism that could be developed was limited by the perceived ethos surrounding traditional Public Administration. The area of management or administrative processes is of continuing concern to practitioners but academics fight shy of an area they see as essentially unglamorous. Over the years, the Department of Public Administration has been strong in these areas but it has been reluctant to develop them. At the time of my visit, it was overcoming this reluctance and showing an increasing interest in personnel management. This development seems particularly appropriate. Syracuse's strength has lain and continues to lie in the continuing prominence given to management processes in its curricula. Rather than apologising for this traditional focus, emphasising its relevance and importance seems, to this writer, both to build on known virtues - Syracuse has some very good faculty in the personnel and budgeting areas - and to add to the variety of Public Administration degrees currently available in the United States. Other approaches to Public Administration may denigrate this focus but it would be distinctive and the subject matter is of continuing importance. The insidious effect of the NASPAA standards is that they push everybody into doing everthing. But the vast majority of universities, not to mention their students, cannot and will not be able to do it. It may be a trite maxim, and perhaps nostalgic of Public Administration's proverbial

yesterdays, but 'do what you're best at' is the one piece of advice
NASPAA did not offer.   It is the kind of advice which is most
appropriate in the eclectic, multi-disciplinary world of Public
Administration.   The field is too broad to be encompassed in one
degree in one department.

I have criticised the Syracuse programmes for their all-embracing
nature and the imbalance between the inclusive and focused approaches,
suggesting that this arises from an attempt to buttress the departmental
basis of Public Administration.   I have argued further that the
Department should insist that its alleged defects are in fact virtues
and develop its existing specialisms in management processes.   It is
only fair to note in conclusion that the Department was becoming
increasingly aware of these problems and searching for ways to overcome
them.   Moreover, I am conscious that my criticisms may serve to
reinforce the unfavourable image of traditional Public Administration.
It should be quite firmly stated, therefore, that Syracuse is one of
the best universities for the study of Public Administration, notwithstanding the claims made for the new schools of policy analysis.   The
emphasis has fallen on the problems I found at Syracuse because they
raise general issues about the study of Public Administration.   The
inclusive approach stimulated by NASPAA runs contrary, on my analysis,
to the nature of Public Administration.   In an era of eclecticism,
specialisation not comprehensiveness is the order of the day.

(b)   The Institute of Public Policy Studies, University of Michigan

The Institute of Public Policy Studies (IPPS) grew out of the University
of Michigan's Institute of Public Administration, founded in 1914.   The
programme was reorganised in 1968 to emphasise multi-disciplinary work
and 'to prepare students to become part of this expanding public sector,
either as high-level administrators, policy analysts, consultants or
planners'.   Moreover, such students would be the administrative
generalists of the future, possessing 'the most advanced skills in
economic analysis and management science' and an understanding of the
social, economic and political processes of the public sector.(16)   In
1975/76, the Institute offered 5 degree programmes - Master of Public
Policy (MPP); Master of Public Administration(for practitioners);
Joint Law and Public Policy Programme; Master of Science in Public
Systems Engineering (for natural scientists); and a Ph.D. in Public
Policy.   The greatest proportion of students were registered for the
MPP: this programme I examine in more detail.

The MPP was a two year course with a core curriculum of 9, one
semester long courses - Problems in Public Policy, Public Organisation
and Administration, I and II, Public Sector Systems Analysis,
Mathematical Foundations for Optimisation, and Quantitative Methods
for Public Administration I and II.   In addition, one other elective
course in quantitative methods had to be chosen.   Most of this core
curriculum was taken in the first year and some substitution of
electives for core subjects was allowed.   During the second year, the
core curriculum was completed: 2 policy research seminars had to be
chosen from those offered by IPPS (e.g. housing) and 4 electives (12
credit hours)were required, chosen from throughout the university.
Finally, students were expected to undertake an internship to acquire
some practical experience.   A number of students extended their intern-

ship, working part-time throughout the second year whilst completing the degree. To summarise, students took an intensive course in analytical methods and their application in selected research areas and in the field against a backcloth designed to sensitise them to the political and organisational context in which they would work. Less politely, IPPS was described as 'Carnegie-Mellon Mk.II' or 'number-crunching gone mad'. The evaluative component of these remarks to one side, it is certainly correct that the MPP had a very heavy quantitative, analytical orientation. Inter-disciplinary work involved basically two disciplines - political science and economics, both with a strong quantitative bias. Of 22 staff, only 3 did not belong to these disciplines. Exactly the same description could be applied to the courses. The degree of specialisation was quite clear and it was deliberate. It was not without its problems.

One of the problems of specialisation stems from what is excluded - there are always sound arguments for bringing in subject X or subject Y because of their demonstrable relevance. Such arguments acquire even greater force when there are problems with some aspect of the existing programme. And IPPS faced this particular dilemma. The courses setting the political and organisational context fitted uneasily into the programme. Compared to the bulk of the programme, they appeared descriptive, 'soft' or non-analytical and difficult to use in analysing problems. At the same time, there was an increasing concern with the ethics of public administration arising from the Watergate affair. Accordingly, the political and organisational context was pushed into the glare of the spotlight, but the part to be played had a loose script. The consequent improvisation - i.e. revision of syllabi, proposals for new courses, rescheduling of existing courses - did not improve its notices. The balance between the acquisition of skills and the understanding of government processes was changing within the degree. Over the years, the analytical focus had been strengthened and the number of contextual courses reduced. Changes were made virtually every year. Recent developments reversed the trend towards a stronger analytical focus. However, there were no clear objectives underpinning the attempts to increase and improve the political or contextual input. In diluting the analytical skills, was the Institute still training technicians, or was it producing intelligent consumers of quantitative analysis? Clearly, this distinction is one of degree. None of the institutes or schools discussed here produced students unskilled in quantitative analysis. But, equally clearly, students can be taught to very different levels. The distinction was expressed as follows at at the Ford Foundation meeting on the policy analysis programmes:

'Wildavsky questioned whether a full course in statistics should be taught at all - on the grounds that, in his view, most policy issues do not depend on statistics and further that it is impossible to train students to a high level of statistical competence in a multi-faceted program. The rejoinder was, that, of course, there are limitations to statistics and students are simply taught the basic uses and abuses of statistics - so as to be intelligent consumers. The tension between training sophisticated technicians as against intelligent consumers was sharply expressed here.'(17)

If the Institute was to increase the contextual input, what were the implications for the rest of the curriculum? Could 7 out of the 10 core courses remain analytical and quantitative? Just what degree of sophistication in the use of the various techniques was expected from the students? These questions constitute the hidden agenda for change because, at the time of my visit, they had not been directly confronted.

This problem was compounded by the rather idiosyncratic nature of IPPS's organisational and staffing arrangements. First, IPPS as an institution was not wholly dependent on its degrees and fee income for its survival. Within the university, it played the important role of enabling the departments either to recruit promising faculty or to provide research opportunities or quasi-sabbaticals for senior faculty by offering salary increments and lighter teaching loads. This recruiting/professional development role was valued in its own right by the university departments independently of any teaching that might be carried out on the MPP. Second, but related to the first point, IPPS had no independent faculty of its own. This had a number of important consequences. Faculty were not necessarily committed to IPPS and its independent work programme. They could remain oriented to their disciplinary department and to personal research. Given these inhibitions to institutional loyalty, the Director of IPPS faced an unenviable task in motivating and energising his organisation - a problem compounded by a third factor. Recent years had seen two new incumbents of the post of Director. This lack of continuity had perhaps delayed innovations. An established Director would have been in a stronger position to affect changes in Institute policy and to command commitment from its faculty. Fourth, the departmental and personal research orientation of staff, despite directoral encouragement to the contrary, limited staff involvement in consultancy. This academic or pure research rather than policy analysis orientation limited the capability of IPPS to offer specialist, problem-oriented policy analysis courses and research seminars. There was a tendency, therefore, for second year students on the MPP to take a shopping-bag around the university for their electives. Finally, the strong links with departments, coupled with the strained relations generated with parts of the university at the inception of IPPS, limited the extent of inter-disciplinary work which was confined largely to contributions from political science and economics. In particular, it limited the inputs from the quantitative aspects of management science and from organisation theory.

If the reader feels that the foregoing indicates a formidable list of obstacles, I have succeeded in conveying my major impression of the IPPS programme. I doubt if I could have invented a much more daunting list. It would be a mistake, however, to suggest that my account would command unanimity at IPPS. The first Director, Pat Crecine, has pointed out that with joint appointments the disciplinary department plays a useful 'quality control function.'(18) The current Director, Jack Walker, would argue that I have under-estimated the extent to which changes were under way to deal with the problems. In my interviews with him, he emphasised the effort to increase staff commitment by appointing 'area' heads (e.g. urbanism, evaluation) to develop the specialisms through research, teaching and consultancy; the intensive efforts, in consultation with students, to revise the political or contextual inputs; the recruitment of new staff to build up IPPS's research; and the end of the inter-regnum period between the first and the current director. I accept that Jack Walker was beginning to stamp his aspirations on IPPS and this development should serve to clarify some of the problems extant at the time of my visit. Nonetheless, two issues are of prime importance - the shift from the acquisition of skills to an understanding of government processes, and the absence of control over staff recruitment and promotion. The reform proposals under discussion at the time of visit did not seem adequate to deal with these issues.

The distinctions between analytical and contextual subjects and between sophisticated technicians and intelligent consumers of quantitative analysis are not just a question of balance: of a mix of the various perspectives. The differences in perspectives have a disciplinary base and, most importantly, they are based on different conceptions of the decision-making process. It is a conflict between the rational and the political models of decision-making and there is no easy solution to it. There is no integrating theory of decision-making. To increase the emphasis on contextual subjects is, therefore, to heighten the conflict between the rational and political models. Integration could occur, of course in the research seminars or work-shops but, as indicated alread, IPPS conceded it was weak in this area and the possibilities of integration are reduced when students develop their expertise in the analysis of substantive policy areas in other university departments. Increasing the political input was, therefore, a challenge to the basis of the MPP. In essence, it was a shift from training technicians to producing consumers of quantitative analysis. It raised the question, not of revising, but of redesigning the curriculum. The reform debate in IPPS did not fully recognise the extent of the changes which could follow from increasing the contextual input. In so saying, I am not necessarily implying that a curriculum must be based on one or other model of decision-making, only that, if both models figure prominently, the conflict between them must be handled explicitly and systematically. IPPS' ability to follow this latter course of action was hampered by its organisational problems.

The organisational problem was not simply a question of having at least some of ones own staff. Unless the vast majority of staff come to see their future in IPPS, it will not be possible to get a coherent approach, a consistency of direction, within the Institute. And such coherence will be essential if the conflict between the rational and political models is to be handled in a systematic way. My reading of the IPPS situation is that the focus on analytical courses and the training of sophisticated technicians was deeply imbued in many faculty. This focus should remain unless there is a genuine effort to redesign the curriculum on the part of the majority of staff whose career aspirations are firmly located in IPPS.

At Michigan, as at Syracuse, the pressure for a more inclusive curriculum exerted a pernicious effect. If it ignored these pressures, IPPS could continue to have a distinctive, analytical focus which is both taught well and appreciated by the students. 'Do what you do best' is again the most apposite conclusion.

(c) Graduate School of Public Policy, University of California,
     Berkeley

Many of the issues raised in my discussion of IPPS are relevant to a
discusion of the Graduate School of Public Policy (GSPP).   The
solutions to the analytical/contextual and the consumers/technicians
distinctions, and to the organisational issues were, however, very
different ones.

GSPP was established in 1968, its first dean was appointed in 1969
and it acquired its current name in 1971.   The name was changed from
public affairs to public policy because, according to a much loved
and often recounted local story which is no doubt apocryphal, 'affairs
are private but policies are public.'(19)

As at IPPS there was a core curriculum in the first year, although
in this case there were no electives.   The subjects taken by students
were: Methods of Social Enquiry; Economic Analysis of Public Policy;
Political and Organisational Aspects of Public Policy; Modelling and
Quantitative Analysis; Law and Public Policy; and introduction to
Policy Analysis.   In the summer between the first and second years
students have to go on a placement or policy analysis apprenticeship.
In the second year, there was one compulsory course, Advanced Policy
Analysis, which included the preparation of a major piece of policy
analysis equivalent to a dissertation.   In addition, students chose
6 electives (or 24 course units) from those available in GSPP and in
the University.   GSPP faculty offered between them 33 electives
covering such diverse topics as The Analysis of Social Surveys,
Population and Public Policy, Poverty and Welfare Reform, Policy
Issues in Communication, Organisational Strategies and Public Policy,
Advanced Quantitative Models, Issues in Mental Health Policy, Law and
Social Change, and Budgets as Political Instruments.(20)   This range
of specialisms was paralleled by the range of disciplines of the
faculty, which included 4 political scientists, 3 economists, 3
sociologists (including a social psychologist and a sociological
demographer) a lawyer and an organisation theorist.

From this bare description, one might emphasise the similarities
with IPPS - the core courses, the prominence of quantitative analysis,
the placement, specialisation in the second year.   Such an emphasis
would be misleading.   The two schools were very different.   GSPP did
not attempt to train technicians but intelligent consumers of
quantitative analysis.   It emphasised the context of public policy-
making rather than analytical skills.   It taught through examples,
problem solving and doing policy analysis rather than class room
instruction - perhaps the most exemplary feature of the programme.
It was an independent organisation, appointing and promoting its own
faculty.   Last but by no means least, it had a distinctive ethos or
leadership style which gave the programme a coherence and a unity of
direction.   And, perhaps the most pleasant feature of the GSPP, the
ethos led to students and faculty continually falling over one another
even when they were not rushing to the coffee machine.   In some
respects, these differences were ones of degree but taken as a whole,
they led to very different programmes.   They can best be illustrated
by looking in more detail at the project work students carried out.

For the Advanced Policy Analysis course (APA), the student body split up into groups, each member of each group being responsible for identifying two problems for analysis. Every problem suggested by a member of a group was discussed by the whole group. The aim was to have a clear and agreed description of the problems, an indication of possible informants or references on each problem, and, most importantly, a specified client for the analysis of the problem. Having agreed or 'licensed' two problems for each member of the group, these were then vetted by faculty - 'Licensing Board" - and each problem was then sealed in an envelope. A student would then draw on a random basis from the problems prepared by his group. The only limitation was that no student could draw the problems he prepared. From the moment he drew a problem the student had forty-eight hours to hand in his completed, typed analysis. This analysis was then assessed by the faculty member organising the APA, by the real-life client if available, or the member of faculty specialising in that problem area if not, and the problem author. The whole procedure was then repeated, only this time the student had 7 days (5 working days) to complete his analysis.

The rationale underlying this project was both simple and persuasive. Analysis in government has to be completed yesterday, with inadequate information, for a specified client. Students must be able to write cogent, helpful memoranda in a short period of time on virtually any issue under the sun if they are to be successful analysts. They cannot adopt the normal university criteria of excellence for analytical work. The project attempted, therefore, to simulate the constraints in the real world - 'telling it like it is'. I have some difficulty appraising critically this aspect of the GSPP programme because I found it an imaginative and challenging development. It also illustrated some of the major features of the GSPP ethos. With the emphasis on the client, the lack of information and of time, the APA project illustrated the tenet that the scope for rationality in government is limited. The emphasis fell on the constraints surrounding analysis and on being practical. The situation was taken as given. The problem was how to work with and in that situation. The concepts of zero-based reviews, of comprehensiveness and of search for alternatives was given a lower priority than the concept of client need, selectivity in the face of scarce time and information, and pragmatism. Allied to these features was the general tenet that you can't define policy analysis, you do it. The APA project exemplified this tenet - it was a tough exercise in policy analysis. But it meant also that there were no criteria for policy analysis other than those of the specific situation in which it was actually done. Good analysis was that which was useful to a particular client with a particular problem in a particular situation. There were no absolute criteria external to the situation.

Not everyone would accept, however, this purely instrumental role for the analyst. They would argue that the analyst should query his client's values, should serve perhaps the 'public interest'. This contrast between clients, selectivity, pragmatism and an instrumental approach to values and zero-based review, comprehensiveness, search for alternatives and the concern with values should define sharply the ethos of GSPP. The distinction is too sharp. There was some blurring. Ethics and values did intrude. The policy analysis dissertation in the second year provided an opportunity for students to look at broader questions such as the role of government and the nature of its interventions. Significantly few students took this opportunity. The ethos was pervasive.

GSPP was an inter-disciplinary school focusing on both an understanding of the policy-making process and, to employ my earlier distinction, on training intelligent consumers of quantitative analysis. Its ethos stressed a situational ethic (21) which manifested itself in the amount of problem analysis the students had to do. To some readers, my description of the school will fill them with horror. It will be argued that policy analysis cannot ignore fundamental issues of social structure and the distribution of power. Others will read this description and think - 'Ah, yes, Wildavsky's school'. They will nod knowingly. Yet others will prefer a stronger reform ethos, and more analytical training. And paradoxically, others would argue for more basic work on the nature of the policy-making process. The social critic, the professional academic cynic, the rationalist and the behavioural political scientist will all find something to dislike. And each from his own standpoint will be right. I was concerned about the dominance of the situational ethic and the downgrading of the analysis of distributional questions. But in very many respects, all these criticisms miss the point.

The study of Public Administration is highly complex. The number of useful perspectives is legion. No one perspective is ever adequate. It is important, therefore, to be able to distinguish clearly between the various viewpoints. GSPP's perspective was clearly defined. Of the roles available to the social scientist in policy-making, GSPP had heeded the comments of Moynihan and Rivlin and opted for a modest, pragmatic conception of the contribution that could be made. Similarly, of the models of decision-making, GSPP avowed the political model. Curriculum design was heavily influenced by the tentative solutions to these issues. GSPP taught the context and trained consumers of quantitative analysis. If you emphasised the political and organisational constraints on rationality, would you teach students how to implement PPBS? This clarity and consistency is a commendable virtue and stands in stark relief to the ambiguity of purpose prevailing in some other schools.

Aaron Wildavsky has been a major intellectual influence on the development of GSPP but his importance should not be over-emphasised. Organisational factors were important. As Wildavsky has pointed out, the school was established in an era of financial surplus; it was located at Berkeley; it controlled its own appointments and promotions; and it was able to recruit full professors with established reputations. One can only say 'amen' to this list of advantages. But these opportunities were not wasted. A different university could have a policy studies rather than a policy analysis programme, but it could still learn from the experience of GSPP. It is crucial to define ones stance towards either policy studies or policy analysis and to pursue that stance with coherence and consistency. GSPP was an extremely impressive situation for this if no other reason.

If it is accepted that coherence, both intellectual and organisational, is a commendable virtue, one feature of the GSPP strikes a discordant note - the relatively limited emphasis given to organisation theory. The situational ethic of the school emphasised the importance of bargaining and the role of the analyst as a partisan in the decision-making process. Accordingly, one would expect bureaucratic politics, and the various aspects of organisation theory concerned with decision-making to figure prominently in the curriculum. It did not, either at the theoretical or practical levels. Only one-third of one course was devoted to the subject. As noted earlier, political science and economics exercised a dominant influence on policy analysis. GSPP included more organisation theory than a number of other programmes but it still seemed a marginal or secondary component.

(d)   Graduate School of Business, Stanford University

During my stay in the United States, it became clear that the Business Schools were major contributors to the study of Public Administration. Accordingly, I visited the Business School at Stanford University to see their Public Management option. Unfortunately, I was there for a relatively short period of time. As a result, my account of their programme is more descriptive and less evaluative than is the case with the other programmes.

Stanford Business School is one of the leading Business Schools in the United States. Founded in 1925, its enrolment in 1975/76 totalled approximately 600 MBA students and 85 doctoral students. As an option within the two year MBA, students could specialise in Public Management and approximately 25 students were admitted to this programme per annum.

The MBA curriculum emphasised management decision-making. 'The study of institutional and organisational behaviour is combined with the study of quantitative techniques and economics to provide a frame-work for analysing problems'.(22)   The public management option differed only in that it extended the core curriculum of the MBA to cover service delivery and conflict management. In the first year, this meant that students had 2 compulsory courses - Urban Political Process and Public Sector Economics - and 2 electives. The remaining 13 courses included Management Accounting I and II, Data Analysis, Introduction to Computer Technology, Decision Sciences I and II, Business Finance, Introduction to Management Information Systems and Marketing Management. During the summer, students were expected to take an internship. In the second year, students took 2 general MBA courses - Business Policy Formulation and Administration, and Business and the Changing Environment - and a sequence of 3 special Public Management courses - Structuring Decisions for the Urban Manager, Decision-Making in the Public Sector, and Public Policy Implementation. In addition, they took 7 elective courses. 32 course were designated as suitable electives for students taking Public Management. They included Urban Finance, Urban Economics, Decision Analysis, Marketing and the Public Sector, the American Woman at Work, Labour-Management Relations, Comparative Economics of Welfare, Transportation Policy, Property Development and Investment Strategy, and Personnel Tests and Measurement.

There were over 100 faculty members at the Business School of whom 22 3 ere actively involved in the Public Management option. Their specialisms included economics, logistics, management science, business administration, educational administration, international economics, computer and information systems, marketing, finance, organisational behaviour and public management.

In brief, the degree programme, the individual courses and the specialisms of faculty strongly reflected the environment of the public management option - namely, its location in a Business School. As a result, there was little political or contextual input, a large input of economics and quantitative methods and, very distinctively, an input of accountancy and marketing. Finally, there was a substantial input from organisation theory - the policy analysis programmes I visited, although they talked of the political-organisational context, substantially ignored organisation theory. Stanford's curriculum reflected a concern with the decision-making skills of that generic animal, the manager. Nor was this curriculum seen as idiosyncratic or irrelevant by employers of the product. Graduates of the public management option found good government jobs at high salaries.

It would be unfair to comment on this programme in any detail. I did not interview all the faculty teaching on the programme, nor was I able to sit in on all core courses because my visit was for two, rather than the usual four weeks. I have described the programme in order to emphasise two points. First, the Business Schools were important contributors to the teaching and study of Public Administration. Second, their programmes were distinctive, emphasising a rather different range of skills and de-emphasising the distinction between public and private management.(23) As I have attempted to argue throughout this paper, notwithstanding NASPAA's pronouncements, each school should identify its singular contribution to the study and teaching of Public Administration. The object of study is too complex to permit only one approach. Stanford had a distinctive approach, teaching that particular range of skills it saw as essential for a manager to be an effective decision-maker. In the past, the Business Schools have been seen as a threat to the discipline of Public Administration. This brief description of Stanford should suggest that the Business Schools offer a complementary approach to that of Public Administration departments and of the policy analysis programmes, whilst none of them has a monopoly over the right way of approaching the subject matter termed Public Administration.

(iv) CONCLUSIONS

The discussion of the institutional forms through which Public Administration is taught has raised a number of issues. The most important of these were:

   (a) the extent to which an institution is multi-disciplinary;

   (b) the extent to which an institution adopts an inclusive approach;

   (c) variations in organisational form; and

(d) the effects of the foregoing on curriculum design/course content.

Many of these issues are closely inter-related, but for convenience they will be treated separately.

Any assessment of the multi-disciplinary nature of the various institutions depends in part on ones frame of reference. NASPAA's frame of reference emphasises the importance of each school having a broad range of disciplines. Their survey demonstrated that such a broad range is limited to an, albeit large, minority of schools. The policy analysis programmes were not limited to a single discipline but neither did they have a very broad range. Economics and political science were dominant. It is, of course, a virtual article of faith for the new policy analysis programmes that they do not cast their subject net as wide as the older schools of public affairs and Public Administration. Certainly, the range of subjects/disciplines was greater at Syracuse. But, cast in this form, it is doubtful that the comparison of the various programmes teaches us a great deal. To begin with, disciplinary labels are an imprecise measure of the variations between programmes. Although it detects some broad differences, it does little more than demonstrate the rather obvious point that no programme draws on one discipline alone. Of greater interest are the many variations within the broad description economics or political science. Moreover, it is not self-evident that the emphasis should fall on the range of disciplines within any single institution. Certainly this range is not the only indicator of the multi-disciplinary nature of Public Administration which can also be assessed by the variations between institutions. Thus, one would conclude that Public Administration was multi-disciplinary if each of the various institutions in the field had different disciplinary bases even though no institution encompassed more than a few of these disciplines. Comparing the different disciplinary 'mixes' of the various programmes does not, therefore, tell us a great deal about the differences between them. A different basis of comparison has to be sought.

A distinction has been drawn between inclusive and focused approaches. The term inclusive has been used to describe institutions which, as a matter of deliberate policy, cover a wide range of disciplines, and varying perspectives within disciplines. This aspiration is embodied in the NASPAA guidelines. The focused approach, on the other hand, selects between subjects and within disciplines to produce a tightly defined and integrated approach to the subject matter of Public Administration. Employing this distinction, it is possible to describe the differences between the various institutions more accurately. Thus, although GSPP and IPPS would appear to have more in common with each other than either had in common with Syracuse, in fact such a conclusion is misleading. IPPS was seeking to broaden the scope of its programme in a way more reminiscent of the older Public Administration programmes than of the new policy analysis programmes. This state of affairs highlights an important problem. The pressures for specialisation are great given the complexity of the subject matter. The pressures to embrace many subjects are similarly great. It is a means of demonstrating ones distinctiveness and, thereby, gaining or

60

justifying separate organisational status within the university. The
subject matter pushes the teacher ever broader in the effort to understand the subject. The penalty of specialisation can be a loss of
understanding. Moreover, it is easier to make the case for including
a subject than for leaving it out. Caught between these twin
pressures, a number of schools had worked out uneasy compromises
embracing both positions. Such compromises would seem to be
essentially unworkable, a point I return to when discussing issues of
curriculum design. At this juncture, I am more concerned with the
implications of this conflict for the future of the new policy analysis
programmes. Just as the discipline of Public Administration sought
resolution of the conflict between inclusive and focused approaches by
specialising either by policy area or level of government, similarly
the new policy analysis institutions will move in the direction of
specialisation by substantive policy area. In fact, Allen Schick has
argued that this movement is already under way:

> 'Over the past decade, policy analysis has diversified ... it
> has broken up into clusters of functional interests. There
> are health policy groups, education policy specialists,
> environmentalists, housing experts, etc. Virtually every
> functional area has its recently established organisations
> and publications.'(24)

He goes on to characterise recent work in policy analysis as 'tireless
tinkering' with policies and programmes. Given the analysis presented
in this monograph, this conclusion should come as no surprise. Lacking
both a clear definition of the role of the social scientist in policy-
making and any core, integrating theory, coherence has been found by
specialising in particular, substantive policy areas. It is difficult
to see how the new policy analysis programmes will avoid this fate.
It is already the cause of much concern in a number of them. At the
intellectual level, I have argued that policy analysis mirrors the
problems of the discipline of Public Administration it has so often
denigrated. Similarly, there is marked parallel between their
respective degree programmes. Both have to make difficult choices
about the focus of their programmes, and both either have or will try
to resolve this problem by specialising in particular policy areas.

Before exploring the effects of this problem further by examining the
detailed implications for curriculum design, there is one further
problem area to be discussed: variations in organisational form. The
relationship between organisational form and programme characteristics
is complex. It is difficult to separate the effects of organisational
form from the effects of other factors. However, from the institutions
I visited, I was convinced that the ability to control the recruitment
and promotion of faculty was of key importance. The disciplinary
bases of faculty exercise a strong influence without being reinforced
by departmental ties. This point is given added importance when one
considers the more general issue of the government of the institution.
When the disciplinary departments are the point of reference for
faculty, it limits the ability of the director to develop a coherent
policy for his institution. His hands are tied by the partial
nature of his staff's commitment to his institution. And there is the
possibility of disciplinary cliques arising within the institution.

Even if, as Mackleprang and Fritschler suggest,(25) there is no
relationship between organisational form and programme characteristics
at the aggregate level, at the level of the individual institution, the
ability to control faculty recruitment and promotion is crucial to
promoting inter-disciplinary work and coherence in programme design.
Reliving the baronial wars of yesteryear does not seem a commendable
strategy.

What, then, are the effects of these various factors on curriculum
design? Two in particular warrant further discussion - the range of
subjects covered and the methods of teaching. Before striking a
critical note, one development should be praised. Recent years have
seen far more attention paid to the teaching of quantitative methods/
statistics. For too long this was a major omission from Public
Administration programmes. The challenge of policy analysis has
corrected this state of affairs. This said, and in spite of the
diversity of approaches to the study of Public Administration, an
examination of the range of subjects covered reveals some curious
omissions. Legal/institutional studies remain 'unfashionable'. The
concern with organisation theory has not led to any great interest in
'bureaucratic politics'.

Legal/institutional studies were once core subjects in Public Administration. With hindsight, the reaction against them during the
'behavioural revolution' of the sixties was understandable but extreme.
To a European, even one from a Common Law rather than a Roman tradition,
their continued omission from Public Administration and policy analysis
programmes is amazing. Studying French or German Public Administration
without studying their constitutional and administrative law is
equivalent to Baskin Robbins selling only vanilla ice cream - it omits
the defining characteristic. I am not arguing for studies of anatomy
alone but for studies of the relationship between the anatomy and
physiology of government. Nor should such studies omit the historical
dimension. How a particular institution or set of institutions
evolved over time can teach much about how public bureaucracies have
adapted to their changing environments. The fate of a particular Act
can teach much about the pitfalls of implementation. The law and the
constitutional framework set the ground rules for policy-making and
implementation and their importance should be given greater recognition
in at least some of the masters' degrees discussed above.

There has been an increase in the number of studies of bureaucratic
politics in recent years.(26) However, given the importance of this
topic for Public Administration, it is perhaps a little surprising that
there have been so few. It is in this melting pot of bureaucratic
politics that the interactions between politicians and administrators
can be most clearly seen. For research, this point does not constitute a recommendation for more case studies. Although the
organisational politics model has been with us for some time, there has
been limited theoretical development. Development of conceptual
models of organisational politics is long overdue. For teaching,
these comments boil down to a simple plea for this topic to be given
greater prominence. The policy analysis programmes in particular are
dominated by the disciplines of economics and political science.
This domination has limited the extent to which organisation theory is
taught. GSPP or IPPS should not necessarily increase their input from

organisation theory, although it would seem to be a logical step for GSPP. However, at least one of the institutions developing policy analysis should be exploring far more extensively the contribution of the organisational model to policy analysis. I did not encounter such an institution.(27)

The most distinctive feature of the teaching methods of all the institutions I visited was their emphasis on accelerated experience. Perhaps the most elaborate example was the project work at GSPP but all the institutions made extensive use of case studies, exercises, workshops and contact with practitioners. The formal lecture, whilst still an important instructional technique, was nowhere near as dominant as it remains, in my experience, in British universities. There was a major difference between the various schools in the way in which they taught quantitative methods and statistics. I described the difference earlier as that between the technician and the consumer of analysis. Obviously, the distinction is one of degree and all the schools produce students capable of carrying out statistical analyses to at least some level of sophistication. Allied to this difference is the difference between the various institutions in the proportion of their course content devoted to contextual subjects as distinct from technical. Both of these differences have their origin in different approaches to policy analysis identified in Chapter 3. Those institutions which emphasise contextual subjects and the training of consumers of quantitative analysis draw their rationale from the political model of policy-making. Those institutions which emphasise technical subjects and skills draw their rationale from the rational model. Where the emphasis falls is not, therefore, a technical one of curriculum design. It is a product of basic disagreements about how we understand the policy-making process. Given the current state of theoretical knowledge, compromise without confusion would seem to be an inordinately difficult task.

This description and commentary upon the institutional forms through which Public Administration is taught has attempted not only to identify problems but also to point to strengths. All of the institutions discussed in this chapter are amongst the leading ones in the United States. All can point to good records in the placement of their students on completion of the degree.(28) My emphasis on the problems of the various programmes should not obscure their very real achievements. In addition, the institutions discussed are but a mere fraction of the total. There are many others, some of which are undoubtedly of a far lower quality than those described above and many of which will have different approaches to the subject matter of Public Administration. But in spite of this variety, I would suggest that the issues raised are common to many of the institutions teaching Public Administration. More specifically, progress in teaching Public Administration is bedevilled by NASPAA's advocacy of a multi-disciplinary, inclusive approach within each institution. I have tried to argue that this approach is harmful and that a subject matter of such complexity requires some degree of specialisation. I have also argued in favour of the diversity which currently exists in the teaching of Public Administration. I have tried to draw attention away from policy analysis. It is fashionable at the moment and 'fads' should not be allowed to hold sway unchallenged. Other approaches

not only have their own intrinsic merits but also they should resist
the temptation to join the bandwaggon. I hope these arguments will
do something to redress the current imbalance in the discussions about
in the discussions about teaching Public Administration.

NOTES AND REFERENCES

(1)   The information on graduate programmes in Public Administration
      is taken from National Association of Schools of Public Affairs and
      Administration, Graduate Programs in Public Affairs and Public
      Administration, NASPAA, Washington, D.C., 1974
(2)   In contrast to the corresponding British survey, the NASPAA
      survey included business schools.   Cf. R.A.Chapman, Teaching Public
      Administration, Joint University Council for Social and Public
      Administration, London, 1973.   NASPAA comment on their survey that
      it 'includes nearly all of the major academic institutions in the
      United States with graduate programs in public affairs and public
      administration'. (p.1).
(3)   A.J. Mackelprang and A.L.Fritschler, 'Graduate Education in
      Public Affairs/Public Administration', Public Administration Review,
      (35) 1975: pp.182-90.
(4)   National Association of Schools of Public Affairs and Adminis-
      tration, Guidelines and Standards for Professional Masters' Degree
      Programs in Public Affairs/Public Administration, NASPAA, Washington,
      D.C., 1974.
(5)   Mackelprang and Fritschler, 'Graduate Education in Public
      Affairs ...', p.189.
(6)   Mackelprang and Fritschler, 'Graduate Education in Public
      Affairs ...', p.189
(7)   The Ford Foundation, Program in Public Policy and Social
      Organisation, The Ford Foundation, New York, 1976, p.5.
(8)   In addition, most of these programmes can be taken in conjunction
      with another programme, especially law, no doubt in recognition of
      the continuing importance of a legal training for advancement within
      American government.
(9)   D.T.Yates, Jr., 'The Mission of Public Policy Programs: a report
      on recent experience', Policy Sciences (8) 1977, p.364.
(10) I know of no survey of all the policy analysis programmes.   The
      data in this section was compiled from a variety of sources including
      information collected on my visits to various universities.
      Additional information was supplied by Charles Wolf (Rand) and
      William Capron (Harvard).   I would like to thank both these
      individuals for their help.   In addition I consulted the following:
      W.L.Dunn, 'A Comparison of Eight Schools of Public Policy', Policy
      Studies Journal (4) 1975/76: pp.68-73; and D.T.Yates, Jr., 'The
      Mission of Public Policy Programs: a report on recent experience',
      Policy Sciences (8) 1977: pp.363-73.   This paper is also available
      as a report entitled Report of a Meeting on Graduate Training and
      Research Programs in Public Policy, The Ford Foundation, New York,
      January 1976.   Accounts of the programmes at a number of individual
      schools have been published in a special, two-part issue of Policy
      Sciences edited by Y.Dror.   See Policy Sciences (1) No. 4 1970:
      pp.401-82, and (2) No. 1 1971: pp.1-85.   A similar symposium was
      published in Urban Analysis (3) No.2 1976: pp.81-281.   Less helpful

because of the brevity of the various accounts is Y.Dror (ed.), 'Symposium on Basic Facilities and Institutions in Policy Studies', Policy Studies Journal (1) No.2 1972: pp.53-103. For some useful articules on teaching policy analysis see W.D.Coplin (ed.), 'Symposium on Teaching Policy Studies', Policy Studies Journal (6) No.3 1977/78: pp.302-392. More generally see Y.Dror, Design for Policy Sciences, American Elsevier, New York, 1971, pp.100-16. For a listing of organisations active in policy studies see The Policy Studies Directory published by the Policy Studies Organisation of the University of Illinois (various editions). However, the listing refers in the main to political science departments. Additional references on the individual programmes are cited below.

(11)   A.B.Stone and D.C.Stone, 'Early Development of Education in Public Administration', in F.C.Mosher (ed.), American Public Administration: past, present, future, University of Alabama Press, Alabama, 1975, pp.30-31.

(12)   The information on the various degrees is taken from the hand-books issued by the Maxwell School. It has been supplemented and amended in the light of interviews with members of the School. See also J.D.Carroll, J.L.Garnett and M.Brostek, 'Public Service Education at the Maxwell School, Syracuse University in a Period of Social Depression', Urban Analysis (3) 1976: pp.159-77.

(13)   At the level of skills, it is claimed that traditional depart-ments of Public Administration ignore analytical and quantitative techniques. The Syracuse programmes show, quite clearly, that such skills are not ignored and the NASPAA guidelines give them similar emphasis. This is but one of the many ways in which the defects of traditional Public Administration are over-stated.

(14)   NASPAA, Guidelines and Standards for Professional Masters' Degree Programs ..., p.3. Commenting upon my remarks about the NASPAA standards and guidelines, Professor Alan Campbell, Dean of the Maxwell School and past-President of NASPAA, wrote:
'My understanding of the role that the guidelines and standards are intended to perform in the public administration education community is different from yours ... It was never intended that every school and program would develop a curriculum which covered the full range of topics and subjects included in those guidelines. Instead, the effort was to define the field of public administration, ... Further, in asking the schools ... to apply the guidelines to their academic program, it was not suggested that they should necessarily cover the full range of the field as presented in the guidelines. Instead, we thought they might relate those guidelines to the areas in which they were specialising.' (Personal letter to the author dated 27 August 1976. Quoted with permission).
However, the guidelines were seen by a number of institutions as defining the goals towards which they should be striving. Moreover, the commentary of the NASPAA report by Mackelprang and Fritschler continually urges the need for individual programmes to become broader-based. Accordingly, I conclude that the NASPAA guidelines were not designed to encourage specialised programmes and that the emphasis throughout is on the development of a more inclusive approach to the teaching of Public Administration.

(15)   For a summary discussion of these issues see L.A.Gunn, 'Six Questions About Management Training', in R.A.W.Rhodes (ed.), Training in the Civil Service, Joint University Council for Social

and Public Administration, London, 1977, pp.10-18.

(16)   As in the case of Syracuse, the general information on the IPPS
programme is taken from the various handbooks supplemented and
amended by interviews with faculty.   See also J.P.Crecine,
'University Centres for the Study of Public Policy': organisational
viability', Policy Sciences (2) No.1 1971: pp.7-32; and J.L.Walker,
'The Curriculum in Public Policy Studies at the University of Michigan'
Urban Analysis (3) 1976: pp.89-103.   Summaries of the various courses
can be found in Appendix A.

(17)   Yates, 'The Mission of Public Policy Programs ...', p.368.

(18)   J.P.Crecine, 'University Centres for the Study of Public
Policy ...', p.22.

(19)   On GSPP see the School's handbook; LeRoy Graymer, 'Profile of
the Programme at the Graduate School of Public Policy, University
of California at Berkeley', Public Administration Bulletin No.26,
April 1978: pp.4-11; and A.Wildavsky, 'Principles for a Graduate
School of Public Policy', Public Administration Bulletin No.16 ,
April 1978: pp.12-31.

(20)   Summaries of these courses can be found in Appendix A.

(21)   This ethic is illustrated by a number of the research
publications stemming from GSPP.   For example, see A.Meltsner,
'Political Feasibility and Policy Analysis', Public Administration
Review (32) 1972: pp.859-67; and A.Meltsner, Policy Analysts in the
Bureaucracy, University of California Press, Berkeley, 1976.   I
should stress that distributional questions are not ignored.   The
point is one of emphasis not omission.   For a corrective to the
emphasis on the situational ethic, see F.J.Levy, A.Meltsner and
A.Wildavsky, Urban Outcomes, University of California Press,
Berkeley, 1974.

(22)   Public Management, Graduate School of Business, Stanford
University, 1975, p.2.

(23)   Obviously, this conclusion is based on my limited exposure to
American Business Schools.   The same conclusion could be applied,
however, to Cornell University's Graduate School of Business and
Public Administration which I visited briefly.   Public management
programmes are offered also by Northwestern and Boston universities.
Further information on the latter can be found in R.M.Weinberg,
'Public Service Education: the Boston University experience',
Urban Analysis (3) 1976: pp.115-24.

(24)   A. Schick, 'Beyond Analysis', Public Administration Review (37)
1977, pp.260-61.

(25)   See p.41. above.

(26)   See for example A.Altschuler (ed.), The Politics of the Federal
Bureaucracy, Dodds, Mead, New York, 1968; F.E. Rourke, Bureaucratic
Power in National Politics, Little, Brown, Boston, 2nd edition, 1972;
and H.Seidman, Politics, Position and Power: the dynamics of federal
organisation, Oxford University Press, New York, 2nd edition, 1975.
Another study which would fall into this category but which is not
of American government is H.Heclo and A.Wildavsky, The Private
Government of Public Money, Macmillan, London, 1974.

(27)   This conclusion refers only to the policy analysis programmes.
Both Syracuse and Stanford offered a range of courses in various
aspects of organisation theory.   Nor should this conclusion be
applied to those schools specialising either by function or level of
government.   As noted earlier, I did not pay an extended visit to

such a school.   Given the argument of this section, it is perhaps
worth emphasising that these schools have made a large contribution
in a number of policy areas.   During the 1960s the 'urban crisis'
led to considerable interest in urban studies.   It has slipped from
the headlines in recent years and the Ford Foundation support for
this development has terminated.   See W.C.Pendleton, Urban Studies
and the University - the Ford Foundation experience, The Ford
Foundation, New York, 1974.   Nonetheless there are still a large
number of schools and programmes in this area.

(28)   For the relevant figures see Carroll et al., 'Public Service
Education at the Maxwell School ... ', pp.171-5, and Graymer,
'Profile of the Programme at the Graduate School of Public Policy...',
pp.8-11.

5 Public Administration and Policy Analysis in Britain

(i)   INTRODUCTION

As in the discussion of American Public Administration and policy
analysis, this chapter first surveys the current state of British
Public Administration - the context - before presenting a case study
of a particular master's degree programme. The description of the
context takes the form of a critique of the 'conventional wisdom'
about the state of British Public Administration. In brief, the
subject is said to have 4 characteristics:

(a)   The absence of a tradition of teaching and research in Public
       Administration in Britain with, as a result, a missing
       literature.

(b)   The prevalence of institutional case studies in the limited
       research carried out in Britain in the post-war period.

(c)   The attachment to politics as the disciplinary base and the
       concomitant failure to draw on the insights of other disciplines,
       particularly economics and organisation theory.

(d)   The limited resources (institutional and financial) available to
       British Public Administration.

Whilst this portrait contains a substantial grain of truth,(1) there
are some important qualifications to be made. There has been an
expansion of the institutional base in the past decade and American
developments have exercised an important influence in stimulating
British developments. This survey strikes, therefore, a predominantly
optimistic note. It does so because there has been a tendency to
ignore recent improvements when discussing the defects of the post-war
period. I recognise that weaknesses remain, but it is just as
important to identify the improvements.

To stress recent changes is not, however, to ignore the very real
problems and difficulties which exist in the study of Public Administration. In turning to examine the master's programme of the
Institute of Local Government Studies, University of Birmingham,
attention is directed to some of these long-standing problems. Thus,
the new degree illustrates at one and the same time both the
innovations which have taken place over the past decade in British
Public Administration and the perennial lack of financial resources
which plagues any new venture.

This discussion of British Public Administration will suggest many
contrasts with American Public Administration. With the exception of
a few passing comments, this chapter does not explicitly compare Public
Administration in the two countries - a task reserved for the next
chapter. However, a note of caution is in order at this early stage.
A comparison of the two countries is fraught with many difficulties.
In each country developments in Public Administration are influenced

by changes in the social, economic and political contexts, and a comparison of the differences at this level would require a book in itself. A full discussion is well beyone the remit of this short monograph. In addition, comparison is further hindered by the lack of research into the development of Public Administration in Britain.(2) This chapter does not provide, therefore, the basis for a detailed comparison of the two countries. The discussion is limited to identifying some of the major intellectual features of British Public Administration in the 1970s and to describing the current institutional base of the subject.

(ii)   'THE MISSING TRADITION'

Professor Ridley has suggested that, in the study of Public Adminis-tration, Britain has been an underdeveloped country – we are the heirs to a missing tradition and a missing literature.(3) For example, British textbooks which contain a survey of administrative theory draw extensively on American contributions but rarely, if at all, on British contributions. It is not self evident, however, that the shift in American administrative theory from classical theory to human relations theory can be used to describe British developments. Moreover, it is too sweeping to suggest that there is no British tradition in the subject. Certainly a number of my American colleagues were somewhat puzzled by the view, and Dwight Waldo commented:

> 'I had never occurred to me to think that Britain did not have an old, honorable, and important tradition in public administration. After all, a great deal of American public administration ... is derived from the British experience. And there was a British Public Administration a decade and a half before there was a Public Administration Review'.(4)

Before describing developments in the 1970s, therefore, it might be as well to start by asking if it is possible to identify a distinctive British tradition(s).

Rosamund Thomas has argued that the American distinction between classical and human relations theory is inappropriate when discussing the development of British Public Administration. Rather the concern with scientific managment and with human relations were intertwined, forming a distinctive philosphy of administration which did not recognise the separation of politics and administration and which emphasised the importance of ethical ideals. Given that such a philosophy existed, it is pertinent to ask why it has not attained greater prominence. Thomas argues that it has not been recognised because the contributions tended to be fragmented both between authors and over the works of an individual author. Moreover, this work often took the form of discursive reflections. There was a lack of what, today, would be called rigorous analysis and limited attention was paid to theory. Even when a recognisable 'school' of thought can be identified – e.g the Fabians – there were as many differences between its proponents as there were similarities.(5)

Thomas's work is a valuable contribution because it challenges the notion that there is no distinctive British tradition. She not only

demonstrates that this British tradition resisted the excesses
associated with scientific management in American, but she also points
to some of its original contributions - e.g. the work on the role of
groups and the human relations aspects of management by the National
Institute of Industrial Psychology well before the Hawthorne
experiments.(6)   In fact, as Rose has pointed out, the quality of the
Hawthorne research would have been far higher if they had drawn upon
the work of Myers and his colleagues at the NIIP.(7)   It is perhaps
hasty to conclude, therefore, that there is a missing tradition in
British Public Administration.   It would be more accurate to talk of
an unsystematic or fragmented tradition but one which, nonetheless,
has its own distinctive characteristics and contributions.

A number of characteristics can be identified in addition to those
discussed by Thomas.   For example, Thomas emphasises the importance of
ethical considerations in the work of many of the contributors between
1900 and 1939.   Her account undervalues, however, the contribution of
the Fabians, and as a result she fails to identify the 'social critic'
component of the British tradition.   The Fabians combined both
descriptions of institutions and policies with an ethical, reforming
zeal.   This concern with describing and evaluating public institutions
and policies has a long history extending from such nineteenth century
notables as Lord Simon, J.S.Mill, Sir Edwin Chadwick and Jeremy
Bentham to recent writers such as Richard Titmuss and William Robson.
It is not limited to the Fabians but they were distinguished heirs to
a long tradition.   The common characteristics of this aspect of the
British tradition are difficult to pin down.   At a minimum they would
include an attachment to 'generalism' - to looking at problems in the
round rather than from a narrow specialist stance - and a commitment to,
and belief in, reform of either politics or institutions - social
engineering.   There is no clearly articulated philosophy associated
with the social critics.   It is a way of working: a stance towards the
subject matter.

This social critic component of the British tradition in the study of
Public Administration has often been confused with a second characteristic - the emphasis on legal, institutional approaches to the subject
matter.   In 1959, André Molitor argued that:

' ... the British have a very definite tendency to reject
the idea of an administrative science per se that would
summarise the substance of the principles that apply to
public administration'.(8)

Over a decade later Professor Ridley was similarly pointing to the
emphasis on structure - the 'Introduction to British Government
tradition' - and bemoaning the lack of 'theoretically-based and
empirically supported' studies.(9)   Finally, Professor William A.
Robson in his survey of the last 25 years of Public Administration
teaching and research in Britain notes that in the 1940s and 1950s:

'The general university approach was essentially institutional.
It concentrated attention on the authorities engaged in public
administration, analysed their history, structure, functions,
powers and relationships.   It enquired how they worked and
the degree of effectiveness they achieved.'(10)

70

However, he goes on to note the increasing emphasis on the administrative process in the 1960s and the growing influence of American
'administrative theory'.   Nonetheless, he emphasises at various points
the continuing influence of the institutional approach with its stress
on the need for 'a firm grasp of the institutional framework of
government'.(11)

The limitations of the institutional approach have been discussed
many times and there is no need to repeat them here.   Suffice it to
comment that a legal/institutional approach is not necessarily
inappropriate or inadequate(13); that it is an important characteristic of British Public Administration; and that the approach is not
invariably associated with the social critic.   Many studies by social
critics adopt a legal/institutional approach but it is not a defining
characteristic of their work.   Its central feature was, and remains,
the desire to describe, analyse and reform.

The argument, therefore, that there is a missing tradition can be
misleading.   It is possible to identify a distinctive British tradition
in the study of Public Administration and the development of this
tradition cannot be explained in terms of the American experience of a
shift from classical to human relations theory.   It is now relevant to
ask to what extent this tradition with its emphasis on a legal/
institutional approach and its emphasis on ethics and values in the
guise of the social critic continues to exist.

(iii)   THE SCOPE OF BRITISH PUBLIC ADMINISTRATION IN THE 1970s

The discussion of the 'missing tradition' in British Public Administration was primarily a discussion of the 'discipline' of Public
Administration.   Many of the critical views cited are by political
scientists who specialise in Public Administration.   But it is
important to distinguish between the subject matter and the
institutional forms through which it is taught.   As was the case in
American Public Administration, many studies of public administration
were in no way associated with the discipline of Public Administration.
The work of the Tavistock Institute,(14) the Industrial Administration
Research Unit of the University of Aston, Joan Woodward, and Tom Burns
had a far reaching impact on the study of Public Administration
although none had any formal link with the discipline of Public
Administration, or departments of political science.   The argument
that there is a missing tradition and literature is only plausible if
the discussion is limited to the discipline which, for much of the
1960s, had limited resources and a limited research output from its
university teachers.(15)   In spite of the 'inadequate base' and the
'over-stretched teaching resources and inadequate research',(16) even
this situation has been changing.

The scope of British Public Administration broadened considerably in
the late 1960s and the 1970s.   These developments are discussed in
this section.   In fact, three developments seem pre-eminent at the
time of writing:(17)

(a) The attempt to evaluate and translate American developments especially in organisation theory, and policy analysis, to the British context.

(b) Developments in organisational sociology which, although pioneered in the private sector, are now being applied in the public sector and which do not explicitly build upon American theoretical developments.

(c) The revival of traditional approaches (e.g. the 'social critic') and traditional foci (e.g. QUANGOs) in the study of public bureaucracies.

(a) Adapting American Developments

R.J.S.Baker has argued that:

' ... the American political environment is so different from the British that American public administration theory is not at all adequate for the British situation'.(18)

Nonetheless, many recent studies in British Public Administration contain substantial summaries of the American literature on organisation theory with comments on its applicability in the British context. Even Baker devotes considerable space to such a summary, and he goes on to offer a typology derived from these theories which he considers more appropriate for understanding British public administration. Similarly, R.G.S.Brown summarises the American literature, arguing:

'A more hopeful approach is to treat the problems(of British central administration) primarily as ones of organisation and to relate them to the ideas of people who have made a special study of such problems as a class ... In studying a problem it is clearly sensible to see what has been learned about similar problems elsewhere. It is also sensible, so far as it is possible to do so, to describe problems in the language and concepts that have been found useful by others, so that common elements in different situations can be identified and related to each other.'(19)

Describing American organisation theory and evaluating its utility in the British context is a useful first step but it is only a first step. It is equally important to adapt these theories by testing them through actual research. Although some useful pointers to research have been identified,(20) not the least by Baker and Brown, the results of such research have not been published as yet. Any final judgement on the utility of American theories must await, therefore, the publication of specific pieces of research applying their concepts.(21)

General reviews of organisation theory are not the only manifestation of American influence. In a less systematic and comprehensive way, policy analysis has permeated British Public Administration. Thus the Social Science Research Council (SSRC) proposed the creation of a 'British Brookings' to develop policy analysis.(22) A number of universities and polytechnics have developed master's degree courses in the area.(23) There is a growing literature. Research into the variations in the patterns of expenditure (if not policies) of local authorities has increased greatly(24) as has the number of publications on public policy-making in general.(25)   More generally, the concern to increase the rationality of government decision-making associated with policy analysis has preoccupied a number of academics, especially economists,(26) and this development has aroused considereable government interest.(27)   PPBS was experimented with, albeit tentatively, by central government and, with more enthusiasm, by local government, under the guise of corporate management and/or planning.(28) Techniques such as Cost-Benefit Analysis, Critical Path Analysis and Management by Objectives have been fashionable (29) although they have been increasingly criticised.(30)   Much of this literature is of an exhortary or of a 'do-it-yourself' nature (31) and there has been little actual research into either the process of policy-making in British central and local government or the effects on that process of the attempts to improve the rationality of decision-making.   It is perhaps premature to offer a detailed assessment of each and all these developments.   A few general observations are, however, in order.

First, the interest in American Public Administration reflects the increased vitality of British Public Administration from the late 1960s onwards.   Second, the diverse nature of this interest coupled with the preference for commentaries over research reflects the limited resource base (institutional and financial) of British Public Administration. Although a number of institutes or centres have been created, their presence has not yet made a great impression in terms of research and publications.   There is one caveat to this point.   The new institutes have undertaken research into a number of areas - e.g. management structures, social policy, structure planning (32) - which tend to be seen as peripheral by members of the discipline of Public Administration.   These members tend to favour studies influenced by political science rather than studies drawing their inspiration from, for example, economics or organisation theory.   Moreover, there is considerable interest in - some would argue obsession with - the role of the administrative class of the civil service.   Both these features tend to limit the range of studies considered to fall within the scope of Public Administration.(33)   The arbitrariness of these limitations is not always recognised.

Third, there is a fine line between selective, sensible adaptation and slavish emulation.   The output studies of local patterns of expenditure seem particularly vulnerable to this kind of criticism. The American studies have been criticised on a variety of grounds including their failure to specify the link between environmental conditions and outputs; the equation of expenditure with policy; the failure to develop measures of policy in place of budgetary allocations; the emphasis on quantitative rather than qualitative aspects of policy; imprecise or inadequate ways of operationalising key variables; and the failure to consider the theoretical significance, if any, of the results.(34)   Although no one study contains all these defects they constitute in total a clear call for careful revision and modification when replicating earlier work.   Unfortunately, the sophisticated methodology coupled with the relatively easy availability of budgetary data tends to drive out these modifications.   The American experience would suggest that, in the second stage, output studies should examine either the influence of organisational factors or explore variations in policy rather than expenditure. Current work does not appear to be moving in either of these directions.(35) Emulation rather than adaptation prevails. It is the ever-present danger when drawing on theories and methods developed in another context.

Four, there are dangers in the scale and sophistication of American Public Administration. Quite simply, it is an impressive venture. The lure of sophistication could drive out interest in traditions. This comment should not be viewed as an outburst of chauvinism. It is but a cautionary note. American political science has been seen to have a substantial ethnocentric component. The utility of American theories in Public Administration has been asserted but not demonstrated. This avenue of development should be explored but not to the exclusion of other avenues. I return to this point in the next section where I examine the contribution of British organisational sociologists. Their contribution is a distinctive one but its applicability to the public sector is not, as yet, widely appreciated. In exploring the utility of American theories, the potential of British organisational sociology, or other indigenous traditions, should not be overlooked.

One final point remains to be made in this section. I have suggested that the concern with increasing the rationality of govern- ment decision-making was stimulated by the development of policy analysis in America. However, there has been an independent British contribution to this development. First, such independent bodies as Political and Economic Planning (PEP) and the National Institute for Economic and Social Research (NIESR) have provided, for a number of years, advice on a range of current issues, especially economic ones. Second, there have been a number of important contributions by British academics in planning and planning theory. It has been a thriving subject in universities and polytechnics for some considerable time and there is an extensive literature associated with it. The original design or architechtonic orientation has declined, in part because of American work in the field, and there have been important research and theoretical contributions over the past decade. The work of the Institute for Operations Research has been important in both these respects but there are many other examples.(37) As already noted, however, this work is denied to Public Administration by its disciplinarians because of the arbitrary criteria employed in delimiting the scope of British Public Administration. The contribution from planning points also to the difficulty in isolating the American influence. All the developments discussed in this section have been stimulated by developments in American Public Administration. In so saying, however, it does not follow that there was no significant contribution from British academics. Planning illustrates the two- way nature of the process of influence.

(b)   British Organisational Sociology

The work of Joan Woodward and Burns and Stalker is widely known in organisation theory.(38) In reply to Professor Ridley's plea for a 'British Crozier', Andrew Dunsire points out:

' ... that Crozier is essentially a sociologist and that the
"British Crozier" (if we need to call them that) is the pair
of Scottish sociologists who three years before The Bureaucratic
Phenomenon published The Management of Innovation. The names
of Burns and Stalker are as renowned internationally as that
of the Frenchman and it is perhaps mere accident that their
investigations were not in the public sector whereas Crozier's
were'.(39)

But if Joan Woodward and Burns and Stalker are well known it is less
commonly appreciated that this work has been subsequently developed
into 'contingency theory'. Again a perceptive quote from Dunsire,
this time from the 1975 and not the 1973 edition of his book:

'Of enormous importance for the development of tools of
organisational analysis was the work of Derek Pugh and his
associates at the University of Aston in Birmingham, comparing
one with another a fairly large number of manufacturing firms
and other organisations in the area by making standard
measurements along dimensions drawn from structural concepts
like size, specialisation, centralisation, formalisation and
standardisation'.(40)

The delay in recognising the value of the work of the Industrial
Administration Research Unit of the University of Aston by the
discipline of Public Administration probably stems from the fact that
their results were available only in articles predominantly published
in America in the Administrative Science Quarterly. The two recent
compilations of these articles should lead to their appreciation by a
wider audience.(41)

It would be a mistake, however, to imply that this work was limited
to the private sector. A number of the original samples in the Aston
research programme included public organisations and, significantly,
found little difference between public and private organisations.   In
addition, this work is being replicated explicitly in the public sector
and a number of research reports have been published already.(42)
More importantly, there have been some interesting theoretical
developments.   John Child has argued that earlier work on the
relationship between the organisation and its environment has been
essentially deterministic. This view, he suggests, is inadequate.
The emphasis should fall on the perceptions of the environment by the
decision-maker and on the ways in which decision-makers choose to
respond to environmental pressure. He posits a view of organisations
in which its goals are the product of a process of bargaining and
negotiation between groups within the organisation. This political
process will result in the formation of a dominant coalition with the
power to commit or withold resources in certain directions. This
'strategic choice' perspective on organisations is an extension of the
'organisational' model discussed earlier and Child's suggestions have
been accepted and are being developed by a number of individuals.
Currently, the approach is being applied in the study of the budgetary
process of English local authorities. It is an avenue of exploration
which has not figured prominently in recent American developments.(43)

Again, it is probably too early to evaluate this development in detail but a few general observations are in order. First, 'contingency theory'although using the social science methodologies developed in America has, at the theoretical level, been predominantly developed by British sociologists and, at least in this case, the process of competitive emulation with American Public Administration has been reversed. A very different strand in organisation theory to organisational humanism forms the basis of this development. British Public Administration is commonly seen to be weaker than, and even inferior to, its American counterpart. In terms of available resources, British Public Administration is relatively weaker but its relative inferiority is more problematic. There is a tendency in British Public Administration to underplay achievements. The contribution of British organisational sociology is better known in America than it is at home. Second, to return to an earlier point, the existence of this distinctive approach to the study of public bureaucracies suggests that developments in British Public Administration need not depend on adapting American theories to the British context. Given the pessimism in the 'discipline' about the state of Public Administration, it is important to challenge the traditional criteria for the inclusion of studies within the rubric of Public Administration and to show that, on broader criteria, there is a distinctive and important British contribution to the subject. Organisational sociology is a base for future developments in British Public Administration.(44)

(c)   Traditional Approaches

Within a framework of limited resources and the growth of interest in American theories, the traditional social critic role has waned. Although work in this idiom continues to be produced,(45) the pervasive influence of American social science methodologies has worked against the reformist orientation of the social critic. Sir Geoffrey Vickers is currently one of the outstanding contributors in this tradition in Britain. The following extracts from a review of his book Making Institutions Work(46) illustrates the unsympathetic response with which work in this idiom can be greeted:

> 'Every era and movement has its sage. From the oracle at
> Delphi through the Roman augurs to the contemporary futurists
> there have been those who have gazed at trends and offered
> their predictions and their warnings ...
> ... he yearns for the golden age of individualism but like
> many before him offers no evidence why life should have been
> so meaningful for the ploughman in the rain ...
> ... Vickers ... is not a man to offer any great measure of
> evidence for his assertions nor is he one to develop all his
> concepts clearly ...
> For centuries the common denominator of oracles and sages
> has been that their messages have been structured in such
> a way that a clear interpretation has only rarely been
> obvious '. (47)

It is conceded that Vickers provides 'inspirational flashes' but the review could not be described as supportive. I do not propose to undertake a detailed summary and assessment of either Vickers or his critics. However, I do want to argue that the social critic approach remains viable even though it is currently unfashionable in Public Administration. In so doing, I am not defending every single piece of work by writers in this tradition. Undoubtedly some writers develop their arguments inconsistently with a cavalier disregard for available evidence.(48)

The complexity of public administration is great and no one approach has as yet demonstrated its ability to comprehend that complexity. In the absence of the approach, specialisation becomes a common research strategy. But greater specialisation creates a correspondingly greater need to stand back and to try and comprehend the complexity in its entirety. It is probably inevitable that such surveys will be lacking in theoretical precision and supporting evidence. Such inadequacies matter less than the success or failure of the survey in identifying inadequacies and omissions in the specialised research and suggesting new ways of conceptualising the phenomena under study. The generalist orientation of the social critic can be justified, therefore, by its ability to re-orient and redirect specialised research.

There are other criteria for evaluating the contribution of the social critic and these are associated with the reformist orientation. Specialised research tends to be descriptive and analytical in orientation, avoiding prescription. This approach is but one way of defining the objectives of social research. Others would argue that research should challenge the society paying for it: the knowledge and skills of the social scientist should be used to change government policies and institutions. There is room for both views of social research and the social critic role is one means of preserving the reformist orientation. But accepting that the social scientist can adopt a prescriptive stance is not to accept the primacy of the polemic. It is incumbent upon the social critic to be clear and precise in his analysis of the inadequacies of government policies and institutions. The predictive ability of social science is very limited and specific reform proposals, because they are predictions, are a matter of political judgement.(49) The evaluation underlying the reform proposals is not so limited, however, and it is the adequacy of the evidence marshalled in criticising the existing state of affairs, and the thoroughness of the analysis of the values and objectives supporting a particular policy or institution, which are key criteria for assessing this aspect of the work of a social critic. If reform proposals drive out evaluation, then we have entered the realm of the political pamphlet and not academic research.

The social critic is not the only traditional aspect of British Public Administration to survive recent developments. A number of the traditional foci continue to thrive. In particular, the study of nationalised industries has broadened to encompass quasi-governmental organisations and quasi-non-governmental organisations - or, more briefly, QG's and QNG's. The extension of 'government by contract' or the growth of the 'Contract State' has prompted a number of studies, most notable amongst which is the three volume Carnegie series.(50) In other words, although British Public Administration has responded to the challenge of developments in American Public Administration, traditional characteristics of the subject as studied in Britain have not disappeared. They may be unfashionable. However, I have attempted to suggest that the British tradition is, in many respects, an honourable one which can continue to make a valuable contribution to the study of Public Administration. It remains one amongst a number of viable bases for the development of the subject.

This brief review of current development in British Public Administration has argued that, as in America, the subject is studied from a variety of disciplinary perspectives. Any evaluation of the field cannot limit itself to the contribution from any one discipline. Political scientists, sociologists, economists all have their part to play. And when reviewed in this light, the suggestion that there is a missing literature seems inappropriate. However, before presenting any general evaluation of the current state of British Public Administration, it is necessary to examine the institutional basis of the subject. At a number of points I have suggested that such institutional support is limited. To what extent has this changed over the past ten years?

(iv)   TEACHING PUBLIC ADMINISTRATION AND POLICY ANALYSIS IN BRITAIN

The only major survey of Public Administration teaching in Britain was that carried out by Richard Chapman for the Joint University Council for Social and Public Administration in 1972. Before examining the master's degree programme at the University of Birmingham, I describe the institutional backcloth to Public Administration teaching in Britain, drawing upon Chapman's survey.(51)

(a)   The Institutional Backcloth

The Chapman survey lists 37 universities and polytechnics offering at least one undergraduate course in which more than 50 per cent of the course content is regarded by the academic staff as Public Administration. Of these only 12 offer 3 or more courses. Only two polytechnics offer an undergraduate degree in Public Administration (Leicester and Sheffield).(52)   Subsequently, B.A. degrees in Public Administration have been introduced at various polytechnics including Teesside and Manchester.(53)   As Chapman is the first to point out, these figures are slightly misleading. Many more undergraduate courses contain elements of Public Administration amounting to less than 50 per cent of the course content. Moreover, a considerable amount of Public Administration teaching occurs on non-degree qualifications - e.g. ONC, HNC, DMA and DMS. But after noting these caveats to Chapman's data, it still remains clear that Public Administration in the universities cannot be classed as a major subject area for undergraduate degrees. Of the universities only Bath, Kent, Loughborough and Strathclyde offer a degree with a substantial Public Administration component.(54)

A very similar picture can be painted at the postgraduate level. Chapman lists 20 universities and polytechnics which offer at least one course on some aspect of Public Administration within their one year taught master's degrees or diplomas. Of these only 9 appear to offer more than two courses.(55)   And, in sharp contrast to roughly equivalent American degrees, these programmes contain few courses in economics or management. Most commonly the programmes emphasise a general course in Public Administration, organisation theory, policy-making and policy-making in a particular policy area. The emphasis on quantitative and analytical techniques so marked in American degrees is conspicuous by its absence in the British programmes.(56)

The under-developed nature of British Public Administration is probably taken as axiomatic in any discussion of the subject. Chapman's conclusions that there is 'teaching of doubtful quality', an 'inadequate base for developing the study of public administration', 'thinly spread resources', and 'little relevant theory or significant original ideas' would, in all probability, command a substantial measure of agreement.(57) Without in any way disputing that Public Administration in Britain could be improved, I would like to suggest that there is the danger of critical evaluation becoming 'self-pity'. In feeling so sorry for the under-developed nature of the subject, one can ignore the very real changes which have taken place. For example, Chapman points to the fact that there are only 6 chairs of Public Administration to support his argument that Public Administration has an inadequate base. He forgets to point out that the majority of chairs in Public Administration are creations of the 1970s and that other chairs, bearing various titles, are held by individuals who view Public Administration as their major specialism. In addition, the faintly apologetic air which surrounds Public Administration in universities is not so prevalent in the polytechnics. There has been a marked increased in the number of undergraduate degrees in Public Administration offered by polytechnics over the last decade - Sheffield Polytechnic was the first to admit students in 1968. Finally, the new master's degrees in policy analysis are wholly a product of the 1970s. In fact, Chapman's survey and its attendant conclusion should be viewed with a mild degree of caution. It presents a static picture and emphasises the contribution of the universities and Public Administration's links with political science. It undervalues the role of the polytechnics and the business and allied professional schools as well as the contribution from disciplines such as economics and sociology. In order to redress this imbalance, the remainder of this section emphasises contributions from the latter schools and disciplines.

Apart from the universities and polytechnics noted so far, there are a number of institutes which specialise either by policy area or level of government. These include the Institute of Local Government Studies (Inlogov) and the Civil Service College, both of which have at least some of the features associated with a staff college. In the general area of urban studies there is the Centre for Environmental Studies (CES); the School for Advanced Urban Studies (SAUS); and the Centre for Urban and Regional Studies (CURS). In the field of social policy, there is the Centre for Studies in Social Policy (CSSP). In the area of economic policy there is Political and Economic Planning (PEP, now merged with CSSP to form the Policy Studies Institute) and the National Institute for Economic and Social Research (NIESR). In the area of defence policy and international relations, there is the Royal Institute of International Affairs and the Institute for Strategic Studies, amongst others. And last, but by no means least of

the various institutes to be mentioned, there is the Public Administration Committee of the Joint University Council for Social and Public
Administration and the Royal Institute of Public Administration, both
of which function as learned societies as well as sponsoring research,
organising conferences and publishing journals - Public Administration
Bulletin and Public Administration respectively. Without suggesting
that this list is comprehensive - it certainly is not(58) - the above
examples should suffice to make the point that the institutional base
of Public Administration is considerably greater than is commonly
appreciated. However, this conclusion requires that Public Administration be viewed as a subject matter which is open to many disciplines
and not the preserve of any one discipline. Two examples should serve
to emphasise this point. Some of the most distinguished contributions
to the study of Public Administration over the next decade have come
from the economists at the Institute of Social and Economic Research of
the University of York and from members of Departments of Social Administration in various universities, pride of place probably going to the
London School of Economics and Political Science.(59)

Finally, the growing role of the management courses in general and
business schools in particular has to be recognised. The Administrative Staff College (Henley), Ashridge Management College, the
London Business School, and the business schools at Bradford and
Manchester all provide some form of training in public sector management. Similarly, there are specialist courses for managers in the
National Health Service (e.g. Leeds, Birmingham).(60) All these
examples should serve to modify some of the more prevalent assumptions
about the state of Public Administration in Britain. Given the range
of limitations noted above and the varied literature on the subject
discussed in the preceeding section, it should be clear that Richard
Chapman, amongst others, is unduly pessimistic - a mood no doubt
generated by his concern for the discipline in the universities. But
taking a wider view of the subject, and pursuing the under-developed
metaphor, it could be argued that the study of Public Administration
in Britain had reached the stage of 'take-off'. The variety of
approaches to the subject and the range of institutions through which
it is studied are considerably greater than is commonly allowed.

Although I have laid considerable emphasis on the improvement in the
state of British Public Administration, this emphasis should not be
mistaken for premature euphoria. There is still a scarcity of
resources. In turning to examine the degree programme at Birmingham
it will be possible to explore in a little more detail some of the
problems which continue to limit the development of British Public
Administration in spite of the improvements of the past decade.

(b)   The Institute of Local Government Studies, University of
      Birmingham

The Institute of Local Government Studies (Inlogov) was established in
1963 with the following objectives:

' ... to foster research in local government at home and abroad,
to build up a documentation centre and library, to provide such
advisory services to governments, authorities and academic

institutions as its resources will permit, to offer special courses to those engaged in the teaching and/or practice of local administration and government and to develop a school of graduate studies and promote in every possible way the academic study of this field and its problems'.

In pursuit of these objectives, the activities of the Institute were divided into two broad groupings - overseas and domestic activities. Each of these groupings was further sub-divided into management training for practitioners, research and graduate studies. This account of the activities of the Institute is limited to graduate studies on the domestic or 'British side'.(61)

Prior to 1972/3 graduate activities did not have a high priority within the Institute. The number of students had grown slightly to about 10 students per annum, both full time and part time. Most of these were registered for the M.Soc.Sc. by examination and dissertation and there were few students registered for research degrees. The number of applicants was rising, however, and it was clear that the graduate school could grow appreciably in size.

The increase in numbers took place unexpectedly. The University of Birmingham established a Health Services Management Centre as part of its plans to develop post-experience work in the public sector. The Centre has a small number of masters' students and they were registered with the Department of Local Government and Administration - i.e. the Institute in its guise as a university department.(62) This development had two consequences. First, it broadened the focus of the degree from local government to the public sector. Second, it meant that there would be an increase in the number of students irrespective of the Institute's recruitment policy. Allied to the fact that, for once, all the students accepted actually registered,(63) the Institute found itself with 23 full time and part time students. This growth in student numbers posed the issue of the reform of the degree in very concrete terms.

It would be a mistake to give the impression that the problems surrounding masters' teaching had been neither identified nor discussed before the sudden upsurge in student numbers. Previous students had made 'suggestions' about the course. A seminar held at the Institute by Professor Y.Dror stimulated interest and enthusiasm amongst some members of staff in the development of the degree. Discussions had been under way for most of 1972. The increase in the number of students served to translate discussions into action.

Two of the problems identified were specific to the old masters' programme - namely, the overlap between courses and the profusion and growth in the number of courses. Neither of these problems was, I suspect, peculiar to the Institute. The tradition in British universities of allowing staff to present masters' courses in their 'pet' subject remains strong. The result of this tradition at the Institute was a long list of courses, the rationale of which was less than obvious. Internal consistency and planned development came a poor second to staff interests and specialisms. The Institute was in the position of offering 8 courses to approximately 10 students

and 4 of these courses were in the area of organisation theory.
In addition, there was a proposal for a new course and discussions
about two other courses were already under way. This proliferation
had led to a situation where courses were being offered for 2
students. Thinly spreading resources in this way was seen as
unsatisfactory - a conclusion given added force by the nature of the
Institute's other work.

Perhaps the key to understanding the nature of the Institute at this
time was the fact that the fees charged for the post-experience
courses were the main source of income. In 1973, of 43 staff
resident at the Institute, only 4 had UGC funded posts. Thus the
Institute had to find the money to cover some 39 salaries plus the
overheads on the UGC buildings it occupied, salaries for secretaries
and running expenses. As a result, the staff time invested in the
degree had to be paid for out of either research funds or short course
derived income. Allied to this financial constraint is a time
constraint. In a normal year the Institute would run 2 ten-week
courses, 24 one-week courses and some 30 one-day seminars for
practitioners. Such courses made heavy demands upon staff time and
resulted in their withdrawal from other activities. It meant that
the degree had to take second place to short course training.

Dissatisfaction with the existing degree coupled with an increase in
the number of students made it clear that some action would have to be
taken. But it did not indicate what action ought to be taken.
Similarly, it is all well and good to recognise the existence of
constraints but there also has to be some idea of what one wants to
achieve. The intellectual basis of the new degree represented
the Institute's response to some of the current developments and
issues in the study of Public Administration, especially in the
United States of America. There was a considerable degree of agreement on the defects of Public Administration. It was felt that too
much attention was paid to the study of structure rather than process
and to the study of particular decisions rather than the macro-policy-
making processes. In addition, there was too strong an attachment to
political science as the parent discipline and a concomitant failure
to draw on the insights of other disciplines. Finally, it was agreed
that far more attention had to be paid to theory rather than to the
historical, legal and institutional facets of the subject. On the
positive side, it was felt that the new degree should be multi-
disciplinary and that it should attempt to translate the findings and
insights of these social science disciplines into terms relevant to
the practitioner. Above all, the emphasis fell on American developments in organisation theory and policy analysis. In essence they
were to provide the twin pillars upon which the new degree would be
built. In reaching this consensus, the range of skills available
within the Institute were an important influence.

The origins of the Institute lie in the Public Administration
teaching of the Politics Department of the University of Birmingham.
This concern with politics was married to a concern with 'management'.
Unfortunately, this label does not advance the discussion very far.
What is 'management'? There is no easy answer to this question, and
no short definition of the term would accurately convey the scope of

interests within the Institute.   Without pretending that the
following description encompasses all facets of the Institute, the
main foci at this time can be said to have been corporate management/
planning and the management structures of local authorities.   These
two areas are but specific forms of the more general areas of public
policy-making and organisation theory respectively.   Other specialisms
existed, including operations research and public finance of the quantitative   subjects and personnel management and social administration
of the more humanistic subjects.   But these latter specialisms tended
to feed into the context provided by organisation theory and public
policy-making.   Not surprisingly, it was relatively easy to reach
agreement in a situation where staff skills and the proposed basis of
the new degree overlapped to a considerable extent.

However, the agreement reached was of a general nature.   The labels
public policy-making and organisation theory can obscure as much as
they reveal.   It was necessary to translate this general agreement
into specific courses.   Thus, the study of public policy-making can
range from a quantitative-analytical endeavour drawing upon a range of
disciplines to the study of essentially descriptive case studies.   The
latter was not, as indicated above, acceptable.   The former was not
possible because the resources were simply not available - the
Institute had no economist specialising in the application of that
discipline to the study of public sector problems.   As a result, the
course focused on policy-making in local government and the National
Health Service drawing upon political science for most of its theory
and research.   If agreeing the general format of the degree proved
relatively easy, translating this agreement into specific courses was
far more difficult and the resource constraints proved somewhat
intransigent.   Before examining these problems in detail, however, the
final form of the degree should be described.

(a)   Compulsory Component

Policy-making in Local Government and the National Health Service.

Organisation Theory in Local Government and the National Health Service.

Project work associated with the above two courses.(64)

(b)   Optional Component

Financial Management in Local Government and the National Health
   Service.

Personnel Management in Local Government and the National Health
   Service.

The Environment of Health and Local Authorities.

Decision Simulation.

Other courses offered by the Faculty.

(c)   Dissertation

10,000 words in length and demonstrating 'a capacity to marshall facts and arguments'.   The dissertation had to be submitted within three months of completing the course (December).

As with all the other degree programmes described in this monograph, short descriptions of the various courses are provided in Appendix 1. In addition to the two core courses, students had to select one subject from the list of optional courses.   Thus, of the original 8 courses, only 4 remained and they had been substantially revised.   At least 6 members of staff no longer taught full-weight courses.   The changes had resulted in substantial stream-lining.   The new degree became fully operational in October 1975, although the core courses were taught in the session 1974/5.   And when the degree commenced in its fully-revised form, two additional changes had been made.   First, after prolonged discussion in the Faculty, it was finally agreed that the core courses could be examined through a combination of seminar papers, projects and essay work.   The three hour written examination was abolished.   Given that the majority of students were 'mature' students who had already proved that they could jump through the hoop of examinations, this change was felt to be particularly important by the staff teaching the degree.   In addition, it was argued that, on a course which laid such emphasis on project work (see below), three hour written examinations were at best a distraction and at worst a positive handicap.   Students should concentrate on their written work throughout the year and not be continually looking over their shoulders to the written examinations.   The very existence of those examinations limited staff in the demands they could make on students in terms of course work.

The second innovation was project work.   For most of the past two years, discussions had been under way on its introduction.   It was felt that the degree as constituted paid insufficient attention to particular policies and problems.   Originally it was thought there should be courses specialising in particular policy areas - e.g. health, social services.   However, this idea foundered on the lack of teaching resources, as did the suggestion of designing a general problems paper which would present students with a series of policy problems to work on both individually and in groups throughout the year.   Eventually it was decided that each student would have to complete two projects during the year.   These two projects would be selected by staff, although neither topic would be narrowly defined.   For example, the first project was to have been on the topic of the incidence of need in a particular geographical area with special reference to housing. A 'support' seminar would provide an introduction to specific facets. of this problem area - e.g. the concepts of need and territorial justice, the methodological problems of measuring need, the problems of need in housing and the state of policy in this area.   Students would then select that aspect of the problem they wished to work on. However, before students began to work on their projects, staff were introduced to the system of project work employed at the Graduate School of Public Policy (Berkeley).(65)   In a very short period of time, it was agreed that this approach ideally suited the degree.   As is abundantly clear from the tortuous progress made in designing the project work, staff supported the principle of such work but were uncertain as to the most appropriate format. The Berkeley approach provided the format and, it should be added, was employed with considerable success. Students responded with enthusiasm to the demands that project work made on their time and, even for the short project, the work was to a very high standard.

I have deliberately employed a narrative style to describe the M.Soc. Sc. at the Institute. In this way it is possible to draw attention to the ways in which resource constraints continually impinged upon the new degree. In marked contrast to the American institutions described earlier, there was no Ford Foundation money to support the development of the degree. It had to be designed within known constraints. These constraints included the range of specialists available, the number of staff who could be released for master's teaching and the financial support available for students.

The staffing situation has figured prominently in the above account of the degree because it had unfortunate intellectual consequences. For a programme focusing on policy-making, the absence of a course specialising in the application of quantitative-analytical techniques to public sector problems was, to put it mildly, a matter of some concern. One distinguished visiting professor to the Institute kindly volunteered to lecture to the masters' students and then proceeded to berate them for not taking any economics courses. This problem had already been pointed out to him and it had been suggested that identifying the problem and solving it were two very different matters. It was remarkably difficult to persuade an economist to forswear his natural allegiances and join a non-economics department. Unfortunately, the distinguished visitor did not indicate to the students how economists could be persuaded to join the Institute. But explanations and excuses to one side, the problem existed and, without a specialist economics input, the degree was flawed.

Second, a limited range of options was offered to students. Again this reflected the range of specialisms available within the Institute. To some extent students could overcome this problem by taking courses offered in the rest of the Faculty. However, the integrated nature of the degree and the usual timetabling problems restricted these opportunities. In an ideal world, the programme would have included options in particular policy areas as well as the project work. To employ Dror's term, the degree concentrated too much on 'meta-policy-making' issues and too little on concrete policy problems.(66)

The availability of staff for masters' teaching was similarly a problem. Such teaching commitments always had to compete with other activities within the Institute. In particular, post-experience teaching took priority in a situation where Masters' teaching was making ever increasing demands on staff time - i.e. the project work. Staff input was no longer restricted to one,two-hour seminar and this situation created the temptation to solve the problem of conflicting demands on one's time by delegating masters' teaching to relatively inexperienced staff. Moreover, the degree as constituted was not ideal. There was still a need to develop new courses and revise existing ones - activities which are in themselves time-consuming and, at the end of the day, require the staff to teach the new courses.

Given the demands on staff time, this process of continuous development
assumed a secondary importance.   And these pressures became ever more
insistent as the financial situation of local authorities deteriorated.
In an 'era of inflation' and local authority cutbacks in expenditure,
it became more difficult for the Institute to raise money from post-
experience work and this increased staff workloads.

The worsening financial situation also affected student intake.
Finding funds for students had always been a problem.   The Institute
received only a small number of Social Science Research Council postgraduate awards and, although these increased slightly, they were
never an adequate funding base for the degree.   In addition, there
was usually at least one student on a scholarship from a charitable
trust and a couple of students financing themselves on the assumption
that they would be able to command a better job at the end of the day.
However, the bulk of support for the degree came from local authorities.
They would either second employees full time or release them on a part-
time basis.   By any standards this financial base was precarious and
when local authorities began to cut their expenditure, the master's
degree suffered accordingly.   Student numbers returned to their 1973
level in a very short period of time.(67)   In brief, therefore, the
development of the M.Soc. Sc. at the Institute can be described as
an attempt to adapt American developments in Public Administration to
the British context in a situation of increasingly severe resource
(staffing and financial) constraints.   It is ironic that a degree
which illustrates the recent attempts to develop Public Administration should at one and the same time highlight the perennial
weakness of such ventures.

(v)   CONCLUSIONS

At the beginning of this chapter, I described the major defects
commonly attributed to British Public Administration.   In brief, these
included the absence of a tradition of teaching and research, the
pervasive influence of political science to the exclusion of other
disciplines, the prevalence of institutional case studies in the
limited research output of the post-war period, and the limited
resources available to the area.   In the remainder of the chapter,
I have qualified this analysis in a number of ways.   I have suggested
that if Public Administration is broadly defined to include any
contribution to the study of public bureaucracies irrespective of
discipline, there has been a considerable growth in the range and
amount of literature over the last ten years.   Not only has British
Public Administration been influenced by American developments in
organisation theory and policy analysis but there has also been a
distinctive contribution from British organisational sociologists and
a revival of traditional approaches and foci.   Similarly there has
been a considerable growth in the institutional base of Public Administration with the foundation of a variety of specialist research centres
and the introduction of both undergraduate degrees in Public Administration at the polytechnics and of masters' degrees in policy studies
at the universities.   To sum up all these developments in a single
phrase, I would suggest that the future of British Public Administration can be looked at with guarded optimism.   Although there have

been many improvements, the future of the subject is not assured.
There is still limited financial support available. Without the kind
of funding made available to the American policy analysis programmes
by the Ford Foundation, British developments will remain precarious.

The various qualifications I have made to the conventional wisdom
serve to make the point that British Public Administration has not been
static over the past decade. They are not intended to promote a state
of premature euphoria or to suggest a rosy future is guaranteed.

With the increase in the number of approaches to the subject and the
growing institutional strength of British Public Administration   it
would appear that the differences with American Public Administration
have diminished. The current similarities and differences between
Public Administration in the two countries are explored in the next
chapter.

NOTES AND REFERENCES

(1)   This list of characteristics is a summary of the arguments in
R.A.Chapman, Teaching Public Administration, Joint University Council
for Social and Public Administration, London, 1973; F.F.Ridley,
'Public Administration:cause for discontent', Public Administration
(50) Spring 1972: pp.65-77; F.F. Ridley, 'Public Administration as a
University Subject', Public Administration Bulletin No.11 December
1971: pp.3-15; J.D.Stewart, 'Public Administration and the Study of
Public Policymaking', Public Administration Bulletin No.11
December 1971: pp.42-55; and R.G.S.Brown, The Administrative Process
in Britain, Methuen, London, 1969, p.120.
(2)   The only substantial contribution to the history of Public
Administration is R.M.Thomas, The British Philosophy of Administration, Longmans, London, 1978.   There are, however, a number of
histories of public administration. See, amongst others, G.K.Fry,
Statesmen in Disguise, Macmillan, London, 1969; and H.Parris,
Constitutional Bureaucracy, Allen and Unwin, London, 1969.
(3)   The phrases are taken from Ridley, 'Public Administration: cause
for discontent', p.65 and p.67.
(4)   Letter to the author commenting on an earlier draft of this
monograph dated 20 July 1976.   Quoted with permission.
(5)   Thomas, The British Philosphy of Administration, especially
Ch.2 and Ch.4, pp.146-197.
(6)   Thomas, The British Philosophy of Administration, pp.171-85.
See also C.S.Myers (ed.), Industrial Psychology, Thornton Butter-
worth, London, 1929.
(7)   M.Rose, Industrial Behaviour: theoretical developments since
Taylor, Allen Lane, Harmondsworth, 1975, Chs. 5-8.
(8)   A.Molitor, The University Teaching of Public Administration,
UNESCO, Paris, 1959, p.37.
(9)   Ridley, 'Public Administration: cause for discontent', p.69 and
p.70.
(10)   W.A.Robson, 'The Study of Public Administration Then and Now',
Political Studies (23) Nos. 2-3 1975, p.73.   See also W.A.Robson,
'The Present State of Teaching and Research in Public Administration'
in W.A. Robson, Politics and Government at Home and Abroad, Allen and

Unwin, London, 1967: pp.88-96.

(11)   Robson, 'The Study of Public Administration ...', p.76.
(12)   See for example J.C.Charlesworth (ed.), Contemporary Political Analysis, Free Press, New York, 1967.
(13)   The legal-institutional approach is defended in F.F.Ridley, The Study of Government, Allen and Unwin, London, 1975, pp.25-42.
(14)   See for example E.J.Miller and A.K.Rice, Systems of Organisation, Tavistock, London, 1967. For a critical survey of this work and further references see D.Silverman, The Theory of Organisations, Heinemann, London, 1970, pp.109-24. See also notes 38 and 41 below.
(15)   Chapman, Teaching Public Administration, Appendix 3.
(16)   Chapman, Teaching Public Administration, p.52.
(17)   This section of the paper draws upon R.A.W.Rhodes, 'Current Developments in British Public Administration: some comparisons with America', Public Administration Bulletin No.22 December 1976: pp.54 -74.
(18)   R.J.S.Baker, Administrative Theory and Public Administration, Hutchinson, London, p.186.
(19)   Brown, The Administrative Process ... , p.120.
(20)   See for example the suggestive distinction between administrative, diplomatic and management systems in D.Keeling, Management in Government, Allen and Unwin, London, 1972, pp.91-112. Keeling's approach is sympathetically criticised in A.Dunsire, Administration: The Word and The Science, Martin Robertson, 1973, pp.214-19.
(21)   There has been a substantial growth in the literature discussing administrative theory. In addition to the works by Brown, Baker, Dunsire, Keeling and Ridley cited above, see: P.Self, Administrative Theories and Politics, Allen and Unwin, London, 1972; J.D.Stewart, Management in Local Government: a viewpoint, Charles Knight, London, 1971; M.Hill, The Sociology of Public Administration, Weidenfeld and Nicolson, London, 1972; and B.C.Smith and J.Stanyer, Administering Britain, Fontana, London, 1976.
(22)   See the Times Higher Educational Supplement, 7 October 1976, 22 July 1977 and 16 June 1978.
(23)   See pp.80-87 below and Appendix 2 for further details of these developments.
(24)   For a list of these studies see R.A.W.Rhodes, 'The Lost World of Local Politics?', Local Government Studies, (1) No.3 1975; pp.39-59; and for a critical review see K.Newton and L.J.Sharpe, 'Local Outputs Research: some reflections and proposals', Policy and Politics (5)1977; pp.61-82.
(25)   See for example R.G.S.Brown, The Management of Welfare, Fontana, London, 1975; W.I.Jenkins, Policy Analysis, Martin Robertson, London, 1978; R.Rose (ed.), The Dynamics of Public Policy, Sage, London, 1975; B.C.Smith, Policy-Making in Britain, Martin Robertson, London, 1976; and C.Hood, The Limits to Administration, Wiley, New York, 1976. Rudolph Klein has also made valuable contributions in the field of policy studies although it is predominantly in the form of articles. See, amongst others, R.Klein, 'Policy-making in the National Health Service', Political Studies (22)1974: pp.1-14; and R.Klein, 'The Politics of Public Expenditure: American theory and British practice', British Journal of Political Science (6) 1976 , pp.401-32.   Finally, it is worth noting the emergence of two new journals in the past decade, both of which carry articles on policy studies - namely, Local Government Studies and Public Administration Bulletin - and the

Fontana/Collins Public Administration series of books under the
general editorship of Professor F.F.Ridley.

(26)   Particularly outstanding in this respect is the work of the
Institute of Social and Economic Research, University of York.   See
for example A. Williams and R.W.Anderson, Efficiency in the Social
Services, Martin Robertson and Basil Blackwell, London and Oxford,
1975; A.J. Culyer, The Economics of Social Policy, Robertson, London,
1973; A.T.Peacock and J.Wiseman, The Growth of Public Expenditure in
the United Kingdom, Allen and Unwin, 2nd revised edition, London, 1967;
and A.Williams, Output Budgeting and the Contribution of Micro-
Economics to Efficiency in Government, Centre for Administrative
Studies Occasional Paper No.4, HMSO, London, 1967.   Useful reviews of
the contribution of economists are T.Newton, Cost Benefit Analysis in
Administration, Allen and Unwin, London, 1972; and G.H.Peters, Cost
Benefit Analysis and Public Expenditure, Institute for Economic
Affairs, London, 3rd edition, 1973.
(27)   See for example Committee on the Civil Service (Fulton), Volume 1
Report, Cmnd.3638, HMSO, London, 1972; and The New Local Authorities:
management and structure, (Bains), HMSO, London, 1972.
(28)   For a discussion of the 'new rationality' in central government
see J.Garrett, Management in Government, Penguin Books, Harmondsworth,
1972; and H.Heclo and A.Wildavsky, The Private Government of Public
Money, Macmillan, London, 1974.   For a discussion of corporate
planning/management in local government see R.Greenwood and J.D.
Stewart (eds.), Corporate Planning in English Local Government,
Charles Knight, London, 1974; and J.D.Stewart, The Responsive Local
Authority, Charles Knight, London, 1974, Chs. 1-3.
(29)   See for example J.W.Glendinning and R.E.H.Bullock, Management by
Objectives in Local Government, Charles Knight, London, 1973; M.Spiers.
Techniques and Public Administration, Fontana, London, 1975; and the
various contributions listed in Note 26 above.
(30)   See for example P.Self, Econocrats and the Policy Process,
Macmillan, London, 1975.   For criticisms from a Marxist oriented
perspective see C.Cockburn, The Local State, Pluto Press, London, 1977;
and J. Bennington, Local Government Becomes Big Business, CDP
Information Unit, London, 1976.   None of these critiques match the
analysis in Heclo and Wildavsky, The Private Government of Public
Money.
(31)   See for example, Tony Eddison, Local Government: management and
corporate planning, Leonard Hill, London, 1973; and J.Skitt (ed.),
Practical Corporate Planning, Leonard Hill, London, 1973.
(32)   A complete list of the research publications by the various
institutes and centres would be inordinately long.   The following
references simply give the flavour of the work done.   R.Greenwood,
M.A.Lomer, C.R.Hinings, and S.Ranson, The Organisation of Local
Authorities in England and Wales, 1967-75, Institute of Local Government Studies, University of Birmingham, Discussion Paper No.5, 1975;
R.Klein et al., Social Policy and Public Expenditure, 1974, Centre for
Studies in Social Policy, London, 1974; and D.Donnison and D.Eversley
(eds.), London : Urban Patterns, Problems and Policies, Heinemann,
London, 1973.
(33)   See for example the list of books in Chapman, Teaching Public
Administration, Appendix 3, and note the omission of research reports
on Public Administration whose authors were not members of political
science or Public Administration departments - e.g. J.K.Friend and
W.N.Jessop, Local Government and Strategic Choice, Tavistock

London, 1969.

(34)   See J.Dearlove, The Politics of Policy in Local Government,
Cambridge University Press, London, 1973, Ch.4; B.R.Fry and R.Winters,
'The Politics of Redistribution', American Political Science Review,
(64) 1970: pp.508-22; H.Jacob and M.Lipsky, 'Outputs, Structure and
Power: an assessment of state and local politics', Journal of Politics
(30) 1968: pp.510-38; and S.Rackoff and G.Schaefer, 'Politics, Policy
and Political Science', Politics and Society (1) 1970: pp.51-77.

(35)   An exception to this statement is the work of Bleddyn Davies
which demonstrates a concern with organisational variables.   See
B.Davies, 'Causal Processes and Techniques in the Modelling of Policy
Outcomes', in K.Young (ed.), Essays in the Study of Urban Politics,
Macmillan, London, 1975, pp.78-105.

(36)   A listing of the publications of these two organisations is
simply not feasible in the available space.   For example, there are
21 short monographs in the PEP/Chatham House European Series alone.

(37)   At the theoretical level see G.Chadwick, A Systems View of
Planning, Pergamon Press, Oxford, 1971; A.Faludi, Planning Theory,
Pergamon Press, Oxford, 1973; and B.J.McLoughlin, Urban and Regional
Planning: a systems approach, Faber and Faber, London, 1969.   At
both the theoretical and empirical levels see Friend and Jessop,
Local Government and Strategic Choice; J.K.Friend, J.M.Power and
C.J.L.Yewlett, Public Planning: the inter-corporate dimension,
Tavistock, London, 1974; and D.A.Hart, Strategic Planning in London,
Pergamon, Oxford, 1975.

(38)   J. Woodward, Industrial Organisation: theory and practice,
Oxford University Press, London, 1965; and T.Burns and G.M.Stalker,
The Management of Innovation, Tavistock, London, 1963.

(39)   Dunsire, Administration, p.209.

(40)   Dunsire, Administration, p.115.

(41)   D.S. Pugh and D.J. Hickson (eds.), Organisational Structure in
its Context: The Aston Programme I, Saxon House, Farnborough, 1976;
and D.S.Pugh and C.R.Hinings (eds.), Organisational Structure:
Extensions and Replications, Saxon House, Farnborough, 1976.

(42)   See: R.Greenwood and C.R.Hinings, 'The Comparative Study of
Local Government Organisation 1972-76', Policy and Politics (1) 1973:
pp.213-21; C.R. Hinings and R.Greenwood, 'Research into Local
Government Reorganisation', Public Administration Bulletin No.15
December 1973: pp.21-38; R.Greenwood, C.R.Hinings and S.Ranson,
'Contingency Theory and the Organisation of Local Authorities',
Public Administration(53) 1975: pp.1-23 and 169-90;   R.Greenwood,
C.R.Hinings and S.Ranson, 'The Politics of the Budgetary Process in
English Local Government'. Political Studies (25) 1977: pp.25-47; and
C.Hood, A.Dunsire and S.Thompson, 'So You Think You Know What
Government Departments Are ...?', Public Administration Bulletin No.27
August 1978: pp.20-32.

(43)   See J.Child,'Organisation Structure, Environment and Performance:
the role of strategic choice', Sociology (6) 1972: pp.1-22.   Of more
recent contributions see S.Ranson, C.R.Hinings and R.Greenwood,
Constraint and Choice Within Organisations: the emerging structures
of local government, Institute of Local Government Studies,
Birmingham, mimeo, 1976.   Although the 'strategic choice' perspective
has not permeated American Public Administration and policy analysis
to any great extent, there have been some important contributions by
American academics.   See P.R.Lawrence and J.Lorsch, Organisation and

Environment:managing differentiation and integration, Richard Irwin Inc., New York, 1969; and J.Thompson, Organisations in Action, McGraw Hill, New York, 1967.   For references to the literature on bureaucratic politics see Ch.4 note 26 above.
(44)   Bob Hinings, now at the Institute of Local Government Studies, was centrally involved in the development of 'contingency theory' and, with a number of my ex-colleagues at the Institute, he is now developing the application of the approach to the public sector.   It is possible that my familiarity with this work has led me to over-estimate its importance.   As a result, I have quoted Dunsire at length (note 40) to demonstrate that my judgement is not wholly idiosyncratic.   The sceptical reader could also consider the number of times the Aston articles have been reprinted – see for example, G.Salaman and K.Thompson (eds.), People and Organisations, Longmans, London, 1973.   Even so, my judgement remains open to dispute.   The reader has been warned of possible bias on my part.
(45)   Some of the outstanding recent work in this tradition would include R.M.Titmuss, Income Distribution and Social Change, Allen and Unwin, London, 1962; R.M. Titmuss, The Gift Relationship, Allen and Unwin, London, 1970; P.Townsend, The Last Refuge, Routledge and Kegan Paul, London, 1962; P.Townsend, Sociology and Social Policy, Allen Lane, London, 1975; and B.Abel-Smith, Lawyers and the Courts, Heinemann, London, 1967.   See also the references in note 46.
(46)   See also G.Vickers, The Art of Judgement, Chapman and Hall, London, 1965; G.Vickers, Value Systems and Social Processes, Tavistock, London, 1968; and G.Vickers, Freedom in a Rocking Boat, Penguin Books, Harmondsworth, 1972.
(47)   W.I.Jenkins, Review of G.Vickers, Making Institutions Work, Associated Business Programmes, London, 1973, in Local Government Studies (1) No.2 1975: pp.81-82.
(48)   See for example J.Stanyer's criticisms of W.A.Robson, Local Government in Crisis, Allen and Unwin, London, 1966, in J.Stanyer, County Government in England and Wales, Routledge and Kegan Paul, London, 1967, pp. 8-12.
(49)   There are two ways in which one can evaluate reform proposals – the range and originality of the alternatives and the political feasibility of any given alternative.   On political feasibility see A.Meltsner, 'Political Feasibility and Policy Analysis', Public Administration Review (32) 1972: pp.859-67.   In spite of any advice from social scientists, however, the decision on the feasibility of any alternative remains a matter of political judgement to be made by elected representatives.
(50)   See B.L.R.Smith and D.C.Hague (eds.), The Dilemma of Account-ability in Modern Government: independence versus control, Macmillan, London, 1971; B.L.R.Smith (ed.), The New Political Economy: the public use of the private sector, Macmillan, London, 1975; and D.C.Hague, W.J.M.Mackenzie and A.Barker (eds.), Public Policy and Private Interests: the institutions of compromise, Macmillan, London, 1975.
(51)   Chapman, Teaching Public Administration.   I have also drawn upon F.F.Ridley and D.Steel, University Preparation for Adminis-trative Careers in the Public Service: Britain, Report to the FUCAM Conference, Mons, November, 1975.   The Public Administration Bulletin No. 6 May 1969; No. 11 December 1971; No. 13 December 1972; and No. 19 December 1975 each contained a series of articles on

on teaching Public Administration in Britain. See also M.Starforth,
'Public Administration Studies in Scottish Further Education:
developments in SCOTBEC', Public Administration Bulletin No.18 June
1975: pp.24-29; J.Charlton, 'The Diploma in Public Administration',
Public Administration Bulletin No.18 June 1975: pp.30-33; and
J.A.Edwards, 'The B.A. Degree in Public Administration at Sheffield
Polytechnic', Public Administration Bulletin No.7 December 1969:
pp.25-38.
(52)   This information is taken from Chapman, Teaching Public
Administration, Appendix 1, pp.60-64.
(53)   Ridley and Steel, University Preparation ..., pp.17-21.   On
Manchester Polytechnic see pp.78-79 and on Teesside Polytechnic see
pp.82-83.
(54)   On the undergraduate degrees at Kent and Strathclyde see
Ridley and Steel, University Preparation..., pp.21-22, 73-74, and
80-81.   On Loughborough see W.I.Jenkins and G.K.Roberts, 'Policy
Analysis: a wider perspective on Public Administration', Public
Administration Bulletin No.11 December 1971: pp.57-75, especially
pp.73-75.   There is also an undergraduate course in Public Adminis-
tration offered by the Open University. For a description and
review of the course material see W.A.Robson, 'The Course on Public
Administration in the Open University', Public Administration (54)
Spring 1976: pp.21-30.   Finally, a new degree in Policy-making and
Administration will be introduced by Essex University in October 1979.
(55)   Chapman, Teaching Public Administration, Appendix 1, pp.64-67.
The degrees containing more than two courses listed by Chapman are at
Birmingham, Brunel, Glasgow, Kent, Leeds, Liverpool, University of
London (diploma), London School of Economics and Political Science
(M.Sc.) and Sheffield.   Subsequently, a master's degree has been
introduced at Sheffield Polytechnic.   See Ridley and Steel,
University Preparation..., p.88.   New masters' degrees in policy
analysis have been introduced at the School for Advanced Urban
Studies (Bristol) and at the University of Strathclyde.   For summary
details see Appendix 2.
(56)   The information on course content is taken from Ridley and Steel,
University Preparation..., p.89 Table 2.
(57)   Chapman, Teaching Public Administration, p.52
(58)   For further information see R.Rose 'Resources for Policy
Studies in Britain', Policy Studies Journal (1) No.2. 1972: pp.66-72.
(59)   In particular, I am referring to the work of Professors Peacock,
Williams and Wiseman at York and Professors Titmuss and Abel Smith at
the LSE.   For bibliographic references see notes 26 and 45 above.
(60)   On the business schools see Ridley and Steel, University
Preparation..., pp.28-30; and on health see The Education and
Training of Senior Managers in the National Health Service (Report of
a King's Fund Working Party), King Edwards Hospital Fund, London,1977.
(61)   For details of the other activities of the Institute see R.A.W.
Rhodes, 'The State of Public Administration: an evaluation and a
response', Public Administration Bulletin No. 16 June 1974: pp.27-28.
(62)   The Institute of Local Government Studies is attached to the
Department of Local Government and Administration of the Faculty of
Commerce and Social Science of the University of Birminham.
Technically, postgraduate and undergraduate teaching are carried out
by the Department and post-experience training by the Institute.
The distinction has no practical effect.

(63)   A number of local authorities were committed to sending their
graduate administrative trainees on the masters' degree. In
October they arrived.   In addition, there was always some
uncertainty surrounding seconded and part-time local authority
employees.   Last minute withdrawals were by no means unusual.

(64)   For examination purposes the marks awarded to the student for
his/her project work were allocated to the two core courses.   For
teaching purposes project work was run separately from these courses
- i.e. it had its own timetable slot, teaching allocation, etc.

(65)   For a description of this format see   p. 56   above.

(66)   Y.Dror, Public Policymaking Reexamined, Chandler, Scranton, Penn.
1968, p.8.

(67)   This description of the degree refers to the period 1972-75 in
the main.   More recently, the Institute has acted to mitigate some
of the worst effects of the resource constraints.   For example, with
effect from October 1978, it has created 6 postgraduate scholarships
financed wholly from its own income.

6 Some lessons from America?

At first glance American Public Administration would appear to be superior to British Public Administration in a number of significant ways. It appears to have a coherent intellectual history, a substantial institutional base and a plenitude of resources. For the whole of the post-war period it has seemed to be the source of major developments in research and theory. But this description represents only one side of the coin. As Richard Chapman notes, American students of Public Administration complain of:

> ' ... the widespread lack of resources of all kinds;
> difficulties of staffing higher education teaching
> programmes; the intellectual problem of defining
> what we mean by public administration and of deciding
> whether it is a field of study, a discipline, a science,
> a profession, or the process of conducting public business
> which requires the knowledge and skills of many disciplines
> and professions; and the institutional weakness of public
> affairs schools and programmes compared with other schools
> and disciplines in universities'.(1)

In other words, the same complaints are made on both sides of the Atlantic. The lot of Public Administration would indeed appear to be unhappy. Fortunately, it is not incumbent upon anyone to accept this diagnosis of the state of play. Equally, a comparison of Public Administration in the two countries need not invariably be to Britain's disadvantage. This chapter explores some of the differences between the two countries without extolling either the virtues or the vices of one relative to the other.

As indicated already, it is not possible within the confines of a short monograph to compare Public Administration in the two countries in great detail. Rather discussion is limited to the three topics which have recurred throughout, namely - the definition of the field, the resources available and curriculum design. However, the purpose of this comparison is to identify the lessons which can be learnt from American Public Administration and used to guide the development of this area of study in Britain. In order to draw such lessons from the comparison, it will be necessary, at least briefly, to note some of the differences in the social, economic and political contexts of Public Administration in the two countries.

The first point is· simply the high status of American social scientists in general and students of Public Administration in particular, coupled with the fact that they have been firmly established in American universities for far longer than their British counterparts. To employ L.J. Sharpe's felicitous phrase, a British social scientist going to America is like an English chef visiting Paris.(2) The milieu takes his skills seriously for a change. This difference in attitudes has a number of manifestations, most notably in the way it affects the social scientists' relations with government. The amount of money which the federal government pours into social science research is staggering. And to this one has to add foundation monies and support from state and local governments.(3) The frequency

with which social scientists transfer to important posts within the
federal government is similarly on a large scale. In Moynihan's words:

> ' ... there is no place on earth where the professor reigns,
> or has done until very recently, as in the United States.
> For the past 30 years in our society the intellectuals -
> the professors - have influenced almost without precedent
> in history. The economists primarily (I am leaving aside
> the whole phenomena of the physical sciences), but increasingly
> also the softer social scientists, the sociologists, the
> political scientists and the psychologists'.(4)

Even the most acerbic critic would have some difficulty applying
this description to the 'irregulars' of the Wilson government in
Britain.(5)   Equally clearly, the scale of the American enterprise
called Public Administration is vastly greater than that in Britain.
In terms of numbers of staff, range and number of institutions and the
flow of research and other monies, the difference is enormous.   There
may have been an increase in the vitality of British Public Administration but it does not stand sustained comparison with the American
situation.   I had not expected such a sharp difference in scale but
the contrast was instructive.   First, it placed into.stark and not
entirely favourable relief the upsurge in British Public Administration.   Second, it highlighted the ethnocentric nature of American
Public Administration.   The complaints about the lack of status and
resources and the talk of crisis and disarray betrayed an incredibly
blinkered view of the American scene and an almost total indifference
to the state of Public Administration elsewhere.   Compared to
American political scientists or economists, students of Public
Administration may seem disadvantaged.   When compared to social
science in Britain or many other West European countries, nothing could
be further from the truth.

Allied to the small scale of British Public Administration is its low
status.   For much of the post-war period, the negative attitude of
civil servants towards Public Administration teaching and the obstacles
encountered over access for research have been seen as major stumbling
blocks to the development of the subject.   It was hoped that the
creation of the Civil Service College would improve the status of
Public Administration in the eyes of the civil service.   Unfortunately,
the College has been something of a disappointment to academics,(6) and
the civil service has not viewed it as a success.(7)   The consequences
of this lack of status are more obvious than its causes.   It has
meant that there has been a limited market for the wares of Public
Administration.   The kind of governmental support and encouragement of
Public Administration found in America is muted in Britain.   And as
argued earlier, government demand was an important factor in the
development of policy analysis in America.   Public Administration in
Britain has found itself in a chicken and egg situation.   Its low
status has meant that academic specialists in the area have had a
distant relationship with the government.   But to improve their status,
there was a need to produce quality research which required a far
closer relationship in the form of access to participants and files.

Although the development of Public Administration has been hindered
by the limited nature of government support, the point should not be

overstated. It is commonly made by teachers of Public Administration in politics'departments and the contribution of other disciplines is often forgotten. Certainly the last decade has seen an improvement. Economists and statisticians have become an established feature of the civil service. The 'irregulars' and special advisors, the Central Policy Review Staff, the research programmes of various central departments (e.g. Department of the Environment, Department of Education and Science), the funding of various independent research and training institutes (e.g. the School for Advanced Urban Studies), are all illustrations of the developing relationship between the two sides. But adopting a comparative perspective, it is clear that British Public Administration is the poor relation.

The permeable relationship of government and the groves of academe in America is fostered by the structure of government. The separation of powers and, more specifically, the scrutinising and policy-making role of congressional committees, encourages the employment of professional staffs. The American politician is not a jack-of-all-trades like the British MP. He has his team of aides. As Sharpe notes:

' ... the whole ethos and style of American politics is strongly impregnated with the tradition of drawing upon outsiders as a vital element in policymaking'.(8)

In turn, this situation affects the civil servant. He has to defend his department/policy before congressional committees armed with their own staff and analyses of the strengths/weaknesses of the case being put before them. In addition, the American civil service has a far stronger base in professional expertise. There is no tradition of the generalist 'community' and'village life'(9) at the top. Finally, there is the oft-remarked openness of American government compared to the situation in Britain. To take two small examples, America has the public examination of officials and a Freedom of Information Act.

Any discussion of the causes of the relatively distant relationship between social scientists and government in Britain will, of necessity, be speculative. Nonetheless, it is important to make some provisional suggestions in order to assess the potential for change in the relationship. Sharpe has argued that with the politician, there is a 'very strong sense of self sufficiency'. They do not employ teams of aides and they look to the civil service for policy advice. In fact, to a great extent they see themselves as their own social scientists. For example, the 1964 Wilson cabinet contained 6 former social scientists. Similarly, Sharpe argues that the civil service has ' a sense of omniscience and intellectual security to an extent that is not possible at the equivalent level in the American federal civil service.' Policy-making is dominated by generalists and not by specialists. Moreover, civil servants rarely have to face the critical scrutiny of their proposals by parliamentary committees. The net result is to make the civil service unreceptive to much social science research.(10) Thus, the low status of social scientists, the absence of a tradition of involvement with government, the self-sufficiency of politicians and civil servants and the limited opportunities for employing social scientists all create a situation in which the relationship between the two sides is relatively distant. Without entering such contentious realms as the quality of research done by social scientists in Britain, it should be clear that the reasons for the lack of involvement lie as much in the nature of the British system of government as in other factors. It limits, if it does not preclude, the scope for change. For example, the opportunities for the employment of policy analysts are likely to remain limited because this is a 'profession' offering skills traditionally the preserve of the generalist. There is likely to be a severe and low limit to their marketability.(11) The possibility has to be faced that policy analysis is more a response to the particular needs of American government than it is a requirement of modern government itself.

This excursion into the differences between the social sciences in general and Public Administration in particular in America and Britain has been brief and it has deliberately sounded a note of caution. In exploring recent developments in America to assess their applicability to Britain, it is vitally important to bear in mind the ways in which the subject is influenced by the specific governmental context within which it develops.

In the light of these strictures, it is perhaps as well to start by indicating in what ways the two countries are alike. It is certainly not my intent to argue that Public Administration in the two countries is as different as chalk and cheese. Whatever the difference in scale recent developments in British Public Administration bear a marked affinity to those occurring in the United States - and I am not referring to intellectual fads but the form of the development. In both countries, the subject has developed in a multitude of directions. I described American Public Administration as multi-disciplinary and eclectic. The discussion of British developments shows a similar pattern. There are a variety of specialist centres and intellectual orientations whether one is referring to specialisation by policy area or level of government. Given the complexity and diffuseness of the subject matter, this development should evoke little surprise. Such specialisation is almost inevitable. However, pedestrian though this point may be, its full import is not always appreciated. For some years now the debate in British Public Administration has contained references to the need for a 'centre of excellence'.(12) More recently, the abortive debate about a 'British Brookings' again raised the issue of a single centre. Such proposals run directly counter to the analysis presented here and, although the SSRC no longer proposes to fund such a centre, it is worth noting briefly the objections to it.

However the field of Public Administration ought to be defined, as a matter of fact its boundaries are diffuse and ever extending. In spite of a variety of efforts to stamp a coherence on the field, none have yet succeeded. The problem for any single centre thus becomes one of defining its scope and orientation. To call for a centre of excellence in Public Administration is to say very little. In what areas of Public Administration will it specialise? It will, of course, be multi-disciplinary but which of all the potentially relevant disciplines will be involved? Similarly, a policy analysis or policy studies institute would have no obvious focus. I have argued that policy studies comes in many guises, of which policy analysis is but one. I have further suggested that, even within policy analysis, there is considerable pressure to specialise either by policy area or by level of government. What would be the scope of any single policy studies institute? An all-embracing centre is not a realistic proposal. All that would be created is a confusing jumble of disciplines and topics. In a relatively short period of time, some degree of specialisation would begin to emerge. Nor are the problems limited to defining the scope of any such centre. As Ian Gordon and his colleagues have argued:

'The single hegemonic Institute, totally dependent upon universal acceptability in Whitehall, runs the risk of becoming "over-responsible", cautious and bland.... There will be a strong temptation for a single Institute to assume this Olympian air, and to pitch its analyses and advice at the more elevated levels of the policy system.'(13)

In addition, there is the question of the new Institute's relations with the existing centres. They might not take kindly to the arrival of such a privileged newcomer, and they could certainly argue they already provided the appropriate expertise in particular policy areas. The future of Public Administration and policy analysis does not lie, therefore, in a central Institute. Rather, a pluralistic framework should have been encouraged by the SSRC. There are a variety of existing centres and they should form the basis of development. The subject area is so diffuse that this is the only practical way forward.

This general recommendation runs the danger of simply supporting the present position. In arguing that future development lies in fostering the growth of existing specialist centres, I am not suggesting that all is well with these centres. For example, compared to the situation in the United States of America, there is limited competition between them. An important reason for encouraging a pluralistic framework is this very competition.(14) It is to ensure that a variety of perspectives are brought to bear on the subject matter and to prevent the emergence of any single hegemonic view. In addition, the range of specialist centres remains limited. In spite of recent improvements, relatively few policy areas or functions are covered. Research into central departments in particular remains under-developed. Moreover, where specialisation is the order of the day, there is the danger of insularity dominating interchange. It is important to promote some degree of common awareness of the teaching and research carried out at the various centres. The Public Administration Committee of the Joint University Council for Social and Public Administration and the Royal Institute of Public Administration, like NASPAA, have an important linking role to play in drawing together the disparate strands. But, in order to carry out this role, it is important to emphasise that interchange can not be limited to teachers of Public Administration in the political science departments of universities and polytechnics.

Perhaps the most important problem facing the various centres is financial. Although British Public Administration has, in all probability, a stronger financial and institutional base today than at any other time, as the case study of the Institute of Local Government Studies illustrated, the individual centres nonetheless have limited resources. If a pluralistic, competitive range of specialist centres is to be the model for the future, it is a model requiring far greater financial support than has previously been available. Here, the Ford Foundation's support for the American policy analysis programmes suggests a way forward. The Ford Foundation guaranteed support for a period of 3 (in one case 4) years to a selected number of universities. These twin elements of selectivity and continuity are required in Britain. Now that the Social Science Research Council has abandoned the idea of a single policy studies centre, it should make the funds thus released available to a small number of centres for a period of some 3-5 years. These centres would be chosen to cover a range of approaches to Public Administration. Although it would include existing centres, support would not be limited to them. An important objective would be to extend the range not just to strengthen the existing range. In addition,the SSRC could play a valuable role in promoting interchange between the centres. Through its usual devices of seminars and conferences, it could bring together the various parties on a regular basis.

In spite of the very real differences between Public Administration in Britain and America, one general lesson seems clear. The subject matter is so diffuse that it cannot be contained within a single centre. Future development lies in the direction of a range of competing, specialist centres. If any one feature of American Public Administration is to be emulated, this would seem to be the most important. If specialisation is to be encouraged, the issue of specialisation in what is immediately raised. Are there any developments in American Public Administration which should be directly transplanted into the British context? In what ways can degrees and curricula be modified in the light of American experience? Are there any indigenous developments which should take priority? It is with these more specific questions that the applicability of American experience becomes more doubtful.

The earlier review of organisation theory and policy analysis suggested that their applicability in the British context required a verdict of at least 'not proven'. I also suggested that developments in British organisational sociology and in more traditional approaches to Public Administration provided viable bases of development. Although American developments have been, and will no doubt continue to be,(15) an important stimulus to British Public Administration, they should not be looked upon as the only source of innovation. At the time of writing, policy studies in general and policy analysis in particular, are attracting a deal of attention. As a reassertion of one of the traditional foci of Public Administration this development is to be welcomed. As an academic area of inquiry it is of prime importance. However, as the means whereby social scientists can more effectively contribute to policy-making, it is necessary to be more modest in one's claims. Whereas in the American context there is a market for this commodity, the market for policy analysis in Britain is more limited. There are, of course, some employment opportunities. Corporate planning units in local authorities and planning units in central departments are two possible examples of the employment opportunites open to policy analysts. But these opportunities are limited and the number of policy analysis, as distinct from policy studies, degrees the market can bear will, in all probability, be few. I am not arguing against the introduction of masters' degrees in policy analysis. I am only suggesting that the scope for introducing such degrees is limited in the British context. The study of public policy-making can take many forms which should not be submerged in the clarion call for 'useful' degrees and the 'glamour' of policy analysis. Earlier in this chapter I have suggested that the scope for change in the less than close relationship between social scientists and government in Britain was limited. Putting all of one's eggs in the basket of policy analysis is unlikely to change this relationship. Sharpe's warning is all too appropriate:

' ... an increase in the contribution of social science to policy-making may depend as much on the number and quality of social science academics who stick to their lasts, but take a rigorously critical interest in public policy, as it does on the number who decamp to research institutes and to Whitehall'.(16)

Accordingly, it would be as well to explore the potential of the other bases of development discussed earlier. In reviewing American developments I argued in favour of a focused approach towards Public Administration and policy analysis. 'Do what you are best at' was the maxim employed. The self-same point can be applied to the development of British Public Administration. The British contribution towards the study of organisational politics and organisational analysis has been distinctive, and its application to public bureaucracies offers one of the more exciting avenues of exploration. It should not be swamped by the attempt to emulate American developments.

With the development of policy analysis in Britain placed into a suitable perspective, it is now possible to ask what can be learnt at the specific level of curriculum design. Given the earlier argument, the suggestions made here are necessarily general ones. The reader may perhaps be surprised that I do not have any specific recommendations to make. I have deliberately avoided such recommendations not only because I believe it would be misleading but also, if such specific recommendations were ever implemented, that it would be a terrible mistake. If there are no clearly identifiable, indisputable core subjects which have to be included in all Public Administration and policy studies degrees, it follows that each degree must work out its own emphasis and style. The key criterion becomes the internal consistency of the degree as much as the individual topics themselves.

This caution to one side, there are a number of general features in American Public Administration and policy analysis degrees which seem commendable. First, to an extent that does not occur in Britain, the students are given a grounding in quantitative analysis. Although there are considerable variations in the degree of sophistication expected of the students, all of the programmes I encountered required a certain minimum competence. This kind of technical training is appropriate at the master's level even when staff are critical of the contribution quantitative analysis can make to policy problems. Second, all the courses laid considerable emphasis on 'experiential' forms of teaching, including case studies, exercises, placements and

frequent contact with practitioners. Although these forms of
teaching are employed to differing degrees in British universities and
polytechnics, they do not appear to occupy so central a place. They
tend to be the icing on the cake rather than a substantial ingredient
in the cake itself. There remains scope to explore, therefore, ways
in which these techniques could be more centrally employed. Finally,
and this lesson is negative, few of the American programmes paid much
attention to organisation theory. Admittedly this state of affairs
could be the result of a conscious decision. No programme could
cover everything. However, the frequent allusion to organisational
constraints in the course literature suggests that the omission was
more by default than by design. As I have touched on this issue at a
number of earlier points, there is little need to do more than note
the omission at this stage.

By arguing that certain subjects should be given greater attention,
I immediately place myself in the situation of defining by implication
the contents of any degree in the area. I do not wish to suggest
that every degree should have major courses on quantitative analysis
and organisation theory. To repeat what is the major theme of this
monograph, there is no one, correct way to study Public Administration.
In pointing to commendable features of the American degrees, therefore,
I am doing no more than suggesting possible candidates for inclusion in
a degree programme. The study of public bureaucracies is truly a
crossroads for many disciplines and quasi-disciplines. The challenge
is to define a coherent, focused approach to the subject out of this
melange of approaches. The NASPAA inclusive approach is a mistaken
one.

The lessons to be learnt from the American experience are more
limited,therefore, than might have been thought to be the case. The
context of Public Administration in the two countries is so different
that direct transplants are difficult. Nonetheless, a number of
general lessons have been adduced which suggest possible ways forward
for British Public Administration.

In brief, the survey of both intellectual and teaching developments
in American and Britain suggests the following conclusions:

(a) Public Administration is not a distinctive discipline.
     American Public Administration is multi-disciplinary, diverse,
     eclectic and, compared to Britain, generously endowed with resources.
     The strength of this eclecticism lies in the competition between the
     various approaches to the subject matter. Its weakness lies in the
     ephemeral, not to say insubstantial and faddish, nature of some of
     the approaches.

(b) In spite of the claims made on behalf of policy analysis, its
     most distinctive feature is the extent to which it contains the
     contradictions and inconsistencies of the erstwhile discipline of
     Public Administration. In particular, there is a marked rift
     between those who have a descriptive orientation and those with a
     prescriptive orientation.

(c) Courses in Public Administration and policy analysis vary
     enormously depending upon the definition of the subject matter

employed, the institutional setting and the resources (especially the range of teaching skills) available. There is a marked contrast between those courses which employ the NASPAA guidelines and develop an <u>inclusive</u> approach and those which specialise by level of government or policy area and develop a <u>focused</u> approach.

(d)   British Public Administration has experienced a small but pronounced resurgence in recent years.   In part, this has stemmed from the influence of American developments although distinctive British approaches can still be identified.

(e)   The number of institutions teaching and carrying out research in Public Administration has increased over the past decade but development continues to be hampered, especially in the universities, by the lack of both resouces and government/civil service support.

(g)   The development of British Public Administration in general, and policy analysis in particular, will be best fostered through the establishment of a plurality of competing centres (as in America) rather than through the establishment of a central institution or a centre of excellence.

(h)   Courses in policy analysis should not follow any one format but should reflect the differing skills and ideologies of the various institutions.   However, every single course should contain a substantial 'experiential' teaching component.

Whether the future of British Public Administration lies in emulating American developments or in building on domestic bases, one feature of the subject will remain constant - its diversity.   Public Administration is a frustrating subject.   It offers little in the way of certainty.   Whichever way one turns, a choice has to be made - between disciplines and mixes of disciplines.   The search for the holy grail of disciplinary status is a search for certainty.   The search will continue but it will, in all probability, fail; defeated by the range and complexity of the subject matter.   The diversity of the subject should be recognised as its major defining characteristic rather than treated as a problem.   The future lies in encouraging the diversity rather than in creating the strait-jacket of a central institution. If the pluralistic model of the development of Public Administration is pursued, hopefully a review of the subject ten years hence will view the guarded optimism of this monograph as yet another example of typical British reserve.

NOTES AND REFERENCES

(1)   Richard A.Chapman, <u>Teaching Public Administration</u>, Joint University Council for Social and Public Administration, London, 1973, p.48.   Chapman is summarising the major conclusions of J.C.Honey, 'A Report: Higher Education for Public Service?', <u>Public Administration Review</u> (27) 1967: pp.294-321.
(2)   L.J.Sharpe, 'Social Scientists and Policy-making: some cautionary thoughts and transatlantic reflections'. <u>Policy and Politics</u> (4) No.2 No.2 1975: pp.7-34.   I have drawn on this article in the following

paragraphs and I would like to thank Jim Sharpe for giving me permission to quote from and summarise his paper.

(3)   For example, in 1970 the American federal government allocated £145m. to social science research.   The comparable British figure was £5m.   Quoted in Sharpe, 'Social Scientists and Policy-making ...', p.13.

(4)   D.P.Moynihan, 'The Role of Social Scientists in Action Research', SSRC Newsletter, No. 10 November 1970, p.2.

(5)   On the 'irregulars' see S.Brittan, 'The Irregulars' in R.Rose (ed) Policy-making in Britain, Macmillan, London, 1969: pp.329-37.

(6)   See R.Mair, 'Civil Service Training and the Civil Service College', in R.A.W.Rhodes (ed.), Training in the Civil Service, Joint University Council for Social and Public Administration, London, 1977, pp.41-49.

(7)   See Civil Service Department, Civil Service Training: Report by R.N.Heaton and Sir Leslie Williams,Civil Service Department, London, September 1974.

(8)   Sharpe, 'Social Scientists and Policy-making ...', p.14.

(9)   The phrase is taken from H.Heclo and A.Wildavsky, The Private Government of Public Money, Macmillan, London, 1974, pp.xv-xvi and passim.

(10)   Sharpe,, 'Social Scientists and Policy-making ...', pp.14-15.

(11)   I would like to thank William Plowden of the Royal Institute of Public Administration for suggesting this point to me.

(12)   See for example R.A.Chapman, Teaching Public Administration, Joint University Council for Social and Public Administration, London, 1973: pp.55-57; and F.F.Ridley, 'Public Administration: cause for discontent', Public Administration (50) 1972: pp.75-76.

(13)   I.Gordon, J.Lewis, and K.Young, 'Perspectives on Policy Analysis', Public Administration Bulletin No.25 December 1977: p.34.

(14)   And as Gordon et al., 'Perspectives on Policy Analysis' point out, the Brookings Institution is but one of a number of such policy centres in America (p.34).   The 'British Brookings' proposal is an attempt to isolate the institution from its context.   Amidst this welter of criticism, one benefit from the debate over a 'British Brookings' should be noted.   As Ralf Dahrendorf has argued, the debate 'led some of these institutions (i.e. existing policy centres) to a reappraisal of their ability to do what they had set out to do'. In particular he instances the merger of CSSP and PEP.   See: Annual Report 1976-77, London School of Economics and Political Science, October 1977, pp.65-6.

(15)   One of the areas which seems likely to exercise a degree of influence over the next few years is that of inter-organisational analysis and inter-governmental relations.   On the former see the collection of readings by W.M.Evan(ed.), Interorganisational Relations, Penguin Books, Harmondsworth, 1977; and on the latter see D.Wright, 'Intergovernmental Relations: an analytical overview', The Annals No. 416 November 1974: pp.1-16.

(16)   Sharpe, 'Social Scientists and Policy-making ...', pp.29-30.

Appendix 1 The Core Courses of the Masters' Programme

In Chapters 4 and 5 I listed the titles of the <u>core</u> courses of the degree programmes.   Such titles may not be helpful to readers.   This appendix briefly describes the content of the courses.   It is not fully comprehensive primarily because such descriptions were not always available - courses were being revised and replaced.   I have not included descriptions of elective courses because to do so would lead to an appendix of inordinate length.

(i)   SYRACUSE

Because of the large number of courses offered in both Programme I and Programme II, the following list is only illustrative, not comprehensive.

Examples of Courses in Programme I

Organisational Development (OD):   This course is designed to review the existing literature on OD, to gain exposure to some of the techniques and approaches in use, and to assess its role and applicability to public management.   To the extent possible, class sessions will be discussion-oriented and will incorporate OD exercises so that students can understand and assess OD techniques from an experimental as well as theoretical base.   Some of the key topical areas to be included in this module are: relation of organisation theory to OD; basic concepts and issues in OD; various strategies and tactics of OD; steps in the design of an OD programme; implementation problems; evaluation of OD efforts; case study applications (and misapplications).

Introduction to Government Statistics: This course is intended to help managers interface with statisticians and statistical techniques; to build groundwork for additional learning by students either on their own or through formal work; to indicate where techniques of statistics assist in decision-making, planning and control; to enable performance of elementary analyses; to explore proper and improper interpretation of results, criticism of methodology.   Topics include data errors, data handling, measurement of validity and reliability, error control; descriptive statistics; probability theory, applications; sampling, sampling variability; sampling distributions and estimation, regression, correlation (simple linear, some coverage of multiple, non-linear); introduction to decision-making and time series analysis.

Public Management: The course objective is to understand how the systems concept can be applied to managing an organisation and be a useful tool in monitoring the social conditions upon which a public agency should positively impact.

Political Economy: Topics covered include: 1) nature of the public sector, 2) national income accounting, 3) public goods theory, 4) income determination, 5) benefit-cost, 6) economic planning, 7) federal-state-local taxation.

No prerequisite other than graduate standing.   Students who have had

no previous economics will be expected to read, additionally, an introductory book such as Samuelson, Economics. Usually a mid-term, a
final and some class reporting. No term paper.

Quantitative Aids to Administration: The principal purpose of the
course is to enhance the student's ability to clarify decision
problems, structure their main elements formally, decompose the
problem into manageable components, and reach solutions in terms of
prior decision criteria. The emphasis throughout is managerial
rather than completely mathematical.

Examples of Courses in Programme II

Organisation Theory: Essentially a 'survey course'. The objective
is to achieve a fair amount of knowledge about a vast and varied
literature concerned with the nature of organisations ('what they are',
'how they work', etc.), how they relate to other phenomena (society,
ideology, class, education, etc.), how they can be and should be
'managed' (if they should be), and how they can be and should be
studied. There will be a concern with both empirical and normative
theory.

Personnel and Organisation Development: Prequisite: Class limited
to 30.

   The course will help you learn about OD, get on top of its growing
literature, use and evaluate some of its technology, become aware of
its theory and research, and assess its role in your own approach to
management.

   The following topics have been dealt with in the past; others may
emerge in the forthcoming class.

(a) SOCIAL SCIENCE AND ORGANISATION. The behavioural science view
    of organisations and their culture, systems and their environment,
    change and reality. The theoretical underpinnings of OD.
(b) PERSONALITY AND ORGANISATION. The system and the individual;
    cosmologies of organisational life; learning and growth; motivation
    and productivity; work and play.
(c) ORGANISATION CLIMATE. Structure and leadership; power and
    participation; culture and values; goals and rewards; communications
    and procedures.
(d) ORGANISATION CHANGE. The balance of forces, diagnostic
    techniques, goal setting, collaborative planning, intervention
    strategies, and the technology and management of change.
(e) PERSONNEL MANAGEMENT AND OD. Alternative approaches to personnel
    functions; behaviour modifications; training and development;
    management by objectives.

History of American Public Administration: The course examines the
origin and development of American bureaucratic structures from the
framing of the Constitution to the present day. The impact of
political parties, technological change and social movements upon
government is the major focus. In addition, the role of personnel,
executive-congressional relations, and comparative bureaucracy are
also studied.

Public Budgeting: This course views budgeting as a dynamic activity
that is the focal point of the executive decision-making process,of
legislative policy struggles, and of competition among·clientele
groups.   Areas addressed include the legal framework for budgeting;
the political context; the budget cycle, including budget formulation,
mechanisms for review, and budget execution; the nature of programme
analysis in budget development at the various levels of government,
the relationship of budgeting to planning and management analysis; and
the roles of information and accounting systems as supports to
budgeting.

The course examines financial planning, revenue estimating and
sources of revenue, and the measures available to the executive to
close gaps between expenditures and revenues.   The special characteristics of capital budgeting are analysed, including the interdependence
between capital and operating budgets.   The main historical movements
of budget reform - including programme and performance budgeting and
PPB - are traced and assessed.   The course also reviews the nomen-
clature and mechanics of budgeting, especially classification systems
and the allocation process.   Throughout, budgeting principles and
practices are related to actual cases.

Administrator in the Political Environment: An examination of the
American political institutions affecting public policy and administration and the political environment in which the public administrator must function.   Covers such topics as: Administration under
Pressure, Administrative-Legislative Relations, Judicial Review of
Administration, Executive Responsibility; Bureaucratic Inertia and
the Engineering of Consent.

(ii)   MICHIGAN

Problems in Public Policy: A case approach to elements of problem
structuring, including ethics and norms, quantitative description and
evaluation, the role of theory, projections and design.

Public Organisation and Administration I: The political environment
of public administration, with emphasis on public opinion, voting and
elections, links between elected leaders and their constituents,
relations among legislators, political executives, and civil servants.

Public Organisation and Administration II: Attention is focused on
the dynamic properties of large organisations and the role of
individual decision makers working within them.   Special problems of
public bureaucracies are analysed, including: setting organisational
goals, promoting innovation, leadership, and employee motivation;
instituting policy evaluation and public accountability; and dealing
with legislative oversight and relations with central executives.

Economic Analysis for Public Administration I: Theory of production,
costs, prices; resource allocation; market systems; and governmental
involvement in economic activity.

Economic Analysis for Public Administration II: A continuation of
Economic Analysis I, emphasis on the application of economic analysis
to selected areas of public concern, and a survey of macroeconomics.

Public Sector Systems Analysis: Capital theory and budgeting, discount
rate problems, cost-benefit analysis, estimation of benefits,
distributional and intangible considerations, programme budgeting and
evaluation.

Mathematical Foundations for Optimisation: Functions, set theory,
inequalities, exponentials, elementary calculus, differentiation,
Lagrange multiplier, linear algebra, matrices, vectors, and linear
programming.

Quantitative Methods for Public Administration I: Descriptive
statistics, elementary probability theory, normal and binomial
distributions, sampling theory, confidence intervals, hypothesis
testing, correlation, regression and introduction to statistical
decision theory.

Quantitative Analysis for Public Administration II: Introduction to
operations research; linear programming, dynamic programming, Markov
models, queueing theory, decision analysis, and simulation.

(iii)   BERKELEY

Methods of Social Inquiry introduces students to the structuring of
problems for analysis and to techniques used by several social science
disciplines as they might be applied to the analysis of public policy
issues.   This includes definition of the problem, analysis of the
data, and presentation of research.

Economic Analysis of Public Policy treats the main principles of micro-
economic theory applicable to public policy analysis.   Theories of
preference, of decision under uncertainty, and of production are
examined with an emphasis on the application in the public area.

Political and Organisational Aspects of Public Policy examines the
political and organisational factors involved in developing new
policies, choosing among alternatives, gaining acceptance, assuring
implementation, and coping with unanticipated consequences. Attention
is also given to the ethical dimensions and dilemmas of policy.
Materials include case studies, theoretical, empirical and interpretive
works from several disciplines.

Modelling and Quantitative Analysis introduces the major concepts and
techniques of problem solving from the fields of economics, systems
analysis, and operations research as they apply to the design and
execution of analysis of public policy issues.   The process of
formulating models and interpreting solutions is stressed.

Law and Public Policy focuses on legal aspects of public policy by
exposing students to primary legal materials, including court decisions
and legislative and administrative regulations.   Skills of

interpretation and legal draftsmanship are developed. Relationships
among law-making agencies and between law and policy are explored
through case-centred studies.

Introduction to Policy Analysis develops an understanding of the most
important concepts, problems and roles of applied public policy analysis
through a series of policy problems and exercises. This provides a
common framework for integrating the techniques and perceptions
developed through the other courses in the core curriculum and from the
student's own background. Students also have an opportunity to
develop some facility with collaborative research.

(iv)   STANFORD

Economic Analysis and Policy I and II: The focus of I is on business
decision-making within the firm; on the behaviour of individual
markets reacting to supply and demand forces; on the consequences of
alternative market structures and business policies; and on interactions between the public and private sectors. Specific topics
include supply and demand analysis, consumer behaviour, theory of cost
and production, pricing and competition, factor pricing and the concepts
of marginal analysis.

   The emphasis in II is on the macro, or aggregative, aspects of the
economy. Specific topics include national income accounts, the
determination of the level of aggregate output, employment and prices;
the monetary system, including the effects of monetary policy; fiscal
policy; economic growth; and international monetary economics.

Accounting I and II: A characteristic of business is the extensive
use of accounting and financial data. The analysis and use of
accounting data are important aids to management in the control of
operations as well as in the making of longer-term decisions. I is a
study of the accounting principles, conventions and concepts underlying
financial reporting. Primary emphasis is placed on the accumulation
of accounting data for, and its presentation to, investors. II
presents material on the collection and use of accounting data for
management planning and control. No prior accounting background is
assumed.

Business Finance: This course considers business financial management
and its relation to other functions and to general policy. The
following topics are developed: the finance function; analysis and
budgeting of funds; management of current assets; financing short- and
intermediate-term requirements; and planning of long-term debt policy
and capital structure. Prerequisite: Accounting I or equivalent.

Data Analysis: This six-week course emphasises concepts in the design
of data collection and measurement, as well as specific techniques for
analysing data. Topics considered include: sampling concepts,
hypothesis testing, experimental design, survey methods, regression
analysis and elementary econometrics.

Marketing Management: The primary focus of this course is on
strategic decisions necessary to match organisational resources and

objectives with market opportunities.   Each of the specific strategy
areas of product development and diversification, pricing,
communication through advertising and selling, and distribution is
examined separately, and then according to its role in the overall
marketing plan.   The importance of understanding and forecasting
market behaviour is stressed throughout, as is the coordination of
marketing and other managerial decisions.

Introduction to Computer Technology: This course provides an
introduction to the computer.   Particular emphasis is placed upon
the student's use of the computer as a problem-solving aid.   Topics
include: computer history, hardware and software fundamentals,
essentials of data management and computer programming in the BASIC
language.   Laboratory sessions treat problems in conjunction with
other GSB courses.

Introduction to Management Information Systems: This course focuses
on management applications of computer technology.   Topics include:
designing information systems, evaluating computing equipment,
decisions about computer applications, computers and management
problem-solving, real-time applications and the impact of computers on
both organisations and society.   The emphasis of the course is on
managerial decisions involving the computer and its role in various
information systems.

Decision Sciences I and II: The purpose of these courses is to
develop basic competence and judgement in using quantitative methods
to analyse decision problems.   Symbolic reasoning and methods of
numerical analysis are introduced in the context of several broad
problem areas.   Decision Sciences I deals with analyses of decisions
under uncertainty using the methods of probability and statistical
decision theory.   Decision Sciences II focuses on analyses of
allocation problems using the techniques of mathematical programming.
Although a measure of skill in the techniques of modelling and analysis
is considered necessary for a substantial understanding of the basic
concepts and applications, the major attention throughout is devoted
to the features of quantitative analysis of major significance to a
general manager.

Organisational Behaviour: This course relates existing knowledge of
human behaviour to problems of organisational life.   The course
reviews basic concepts in the following area: individual behaviour,
interpersonal communication and influence, small group behaviour,
intergroup conflict and cooperation, complex organisational behaviour,
relations between organisations and environments.   It purpose, in
addition to providing basic and concurrent knowledge, is to help the
student better diagnose human behavioural problems in organisational
settings and assess the probable human consequences of various types of
organisational change.   The first ten weeks focus chiefly on
individual, interpersonal and small group issues.   The next five weeks
extend the scope to issues of intergroup relationships and design and
functioning of complex organisations.

Business Policy Formulation and Administration: This second-year
course deals with the overall general management of the business enter-

prise. Extensive case studies of a variety of companies of differing size, industry and current condition provide the basis for comprehensive analysis and for the continuous assessment and formulation of broad, basic policy commitments. One part of the course focuses on the planning of corporate strategy. For each company studied, the student is asked to appraise industry trends and requirements; to evaluate the company's present situation and future prospects; to assess potential risks and opportunities; and to plan the deployment of capital and physical resources and the sequencing of company activities for attaining corporate objectives. The emphasis then shifts to strategy implementation - the opportunities and limits in affecting performance throughout the organisation.

Business and the Changing Environment: The primary objective of this course is to examine the increasingly complex set of relationships among business, government, other groups and 'the public'. The course is developed around a series of major current problems chosen to raise some of the major issues involved in these relationships, including an exploration of the development of public policy on such problems. Areas examined vary from year to year. They include such issues as poverty; racial and urban problems; business-government relations through anti-trust policy; the impact of modern technology on business and society; the proper size of the 'public sector'; and the socio-economic responsibilities of business. The course is conducted mainly on a discussion basis. Prerequisities: Economic Analysis and Policy I and II.

Structuring Decisions for the Public Sector Manager: The public sector manager faces a wide range of decisions which are constrained by the complex environment in which he or she operates. The purpose of this course is to develop a framework for structuring information for the decision-maker. In addition, a significant part of the course is devoted to the study of uses and sources of data. This framework includes problem identification and definition, formulation of objectives, and design and evaluation of alternatives.

Decision-Making in the Public Sector: The objective of this course is to examine and evaluate the process by which policy decisions are made in the public sector. This examination includes the way policy issues arise and are perceived by decision-makers, bureaucrats and legislative bodies; organisation for policy-making and planning in the public sector; the types of information, analyses and analytical methods used in the policy process; and the relative influence of political, bureaucratic, economic and other factors in policy decisions. Special emphasis is placed on evaluating the actual and potential roles, contributions and limitations of systematic, quantitative analysis in resolving public policy issues and in developing criteria by which to judge the quality of decision-making in the public sector.

Public Policy Implementation: This course deals with one of the central problems of public management: How do you get things done? Policy and programme decisions often are not implemented in accordance with high level decisions. The reasons for these failures of implementation are many, including lack of technology, conflicting

objectives among key individuals and organisations involved in
implementation, and difficulties of measuring actual outcomes. The
principal purpose of this course is to extend the tools of policy
analysis to include implementation factors and to provide students
with techniques to more effectively translate policy decisions into
action.

Urban Political Process: The activities of public bureaucracies,
both internally and in terms of their outputs, are motivated by
complicated processes. To a large extent, however, they depend upon
how the bureaucracy fits into the local-interest structure, how
coalitions have been formed and may be reorganised within this
structure, and how the power distribution may be shifting within it.
These issues and the role of the decision- maker as he or she faces
them are examined closely through case studies and the academic
literature.

Public Management Workshop: The first 15 weeks of this two-quarter
sequence are devoted to individual and group problem-solving, primarily
in the classroom.   Students work on actual problems of increasing
scope and difficulty as the course develops.   The problems highlight
critical properties of public-sector analysis and decision-making to
include: the use and limitations of quantitative analysis, the nature
of bureaucratic/organisational behaviour, the messiness and complexity
of problems, the effect of structure on outcomes, the intricacies of
coalition formation, and the difference between government patrons/
beneficiaries and clients/consumers.   Regional transportation
problems in the Bay Area and Denver provide the substantive focus for
the 15 weeks.   During the final five weeks each student works on an
individual project for a public-sector client in the Bay Area.   A
choice of topics, clients and faculty sponsors is developed for
students.

(v)   BIRMINGHAM

*The Study of Policy-making in Local Government and the National
Health Service*:   The objective of this course is to provide students
with a theoretical base for an understanding of decision-making and
planning in the public sector.   In general terms, it covers the
descriptive theories of decision-making of such writers as R.A.Dahl,
H.A.Simon, Sir G.Vickers; assesses alternative theories of planning
and surveys existing forms of planning (local, regional, national);
and evaluates recent planning reforms in the public sector (e.g.
corporate planning in local government, PESC/PAR/CPRS in central
government).

Organisation Theory in Local Government and the National Health Service:
The course begins with a critical survey of the development of organisation theory and the contribution of such theorists as Fayol,
Roethlisberger and Dickson, Argyris, etc.   This is the prelude to the
development of a 'contingency theory of organisations' and its application to the public sector.   The emphasis falls on the structural
properties of organisations, their internal dynamics and the relationship between these and the environments of organisations.   Particular

attention is paid to the concepts of 'bureaucracy', 'power', 'organisational culture' (i.e. the relationship between organisational structure and the individual and group behaviour) and 'goals'.

Appendix 2 Recent Masters' Degrees in Public Policy in British Universities

In Chapter 5, I indicated that a number of universities had recently introduced masters' degrees in public policy. This appendix gives brief details of the programmes at the School for Advanced Urban Studies (University of Bristol) and Strathclyde.

(a) SCHOOL FOR ADVANCED URBAN STUDIES, UNIVERSITY OF BRISTOL

With effect from October 1979, SAUS will be offering an M.Sc. in Social Sciences by Advanced Study in Public Policy Studies for both full-time and part-time students. Part-time students will be required to attend the university for 1½ days per fortnight for 36 weeks of each of the two years and for 4 one-week blocks over the two years. The content of the course reflects the School's concern with:

'(i) The study and pursuit of the formulation, implementation and evaluation of policy, combining the <u>substance</u> of policy with the <u>processes</u> of policy-making.
(ii) The comprehensiveness of policy, its complexity, and inter-relationships between policies.
(iii) The importance of inter-organisational relationships in the study of policy-making and implementation.
(iv) Relevance and credibility for the client and for a School in a University with the academic standards that this entails'.

The degree comprises a core course on policy analysis, a special subject chosen from a list of options and a project. Course work consists mainly of supervised reading and research but seminars on research methods and the policy process are also offered. Students are assessed by a written examination in policy analysis, a long essay on the special subject and a formally submitted project report. The project carries 50 per cent of the mark and the written examination and the long essay count for 25 per cent each.

The core course in Policy Analysis covers the context within which policy-making takes place; the various theories and techniques which have been developed to interpret and understand the policy process; the workings of the British political system; and the application of policy analysis to public policy-making. Amongst the specific topics to be covered are the demographic, economic, political, social and spatial changes in urban society; rationality, bounded rationality and incrementalism; inter-organisational planning, influence and power; the allocation and control of public spending; local government finance and central/local relations.

The Special Subject is chosen from the following:

(i) Housing Policy,
(ii) Transport Policy,
(iii) Health Policy,
(iv) Personal Social Services Policy,
(v) Social Security Policy,

(vi)   Land Policy, and
(vii) Employment Policy.

Students will examine the applicability of the various themes, concepts and techniques discussed in Policy Analysis to one of these policy areas.

The project work is intended to draw together the various parts of the course.   It will be an original piece of work, submitted as a dissertation, and it will normally be between 10,000 and 20,000 words in length.   Students will be encouraged to undertake projects which contribute directly to their professional development.

(b)   UNIVERSITY OF STRATHCLYDE

From 2 October 1976, the Departments of Administration, Economics and Politics of the University of Strathclyde have been offering a new master's degree in Public Policy specifically designed for part-time students already in public sector employment.   Students attend for one day per week for 30 weeks each year.   The course takes two years to complete.   The objectives of the course are ' ... to increase understanding of existing policy processes and ... to examine possible approaches to the improvement of public policy-making and policy implementation'.

In the first year students take two compulsory courses: Public Policy-making (Setting, Structures, Processes), and Public Policy Economics (Resource Allocation).   The courses are taught in small seminars and a variety of teaching techniques are employed including case studies, exercises and simulations.   In the second year, students must take 4 classes.   At least one of the classes must be a functional specialism and one an area specialism.   Finally, every student is required to submit a dissertation on an approved subject. The core courses are examined by a combination of written examination, extended essay and class work.   The second year classes are examined by a combination of seminar papers and project work.   The precise allocation of marks for the different forms of assessment varies from course to course.

The aims of the Public Policy-making course are: (1) to provide a framework for the degree as a whole; (2) to trace the development of the 'policy orientation' as a focus for both academic interest and administrative reform; (3) to identify the place of 'models' in the policy sciences and to explore their applicability to the policy process; (4) to examine the concept of rationality in policy-making and to discuss its relevance to different types of situations and problems; (5) to describe and analyse the patterns of policy-making in central and local government; (6) to assess the constraints placed on the policy analysis approach by these patterns of policy-making; (7) to evaluate the various attempts to improve policy-making; and (8) to discuss the emerging role of the policy analyst and the relationship between analyst and client.   Relevant techniques are identified and, where appropriate, taught at an advanced level.

Public Policy Economics is designed to introduce the non-specialist to some areas of economics relevant to policy-making. It does not attempt to provide a 'cookbook' of techniques. Rather, the emphasis is placed on the economic principles which underlie the various techniques and on critically evaluating the techniques. In addition to looking at the economics of decision-making within individual public authorities, the course examines the macro-economic framework within which public authorities must operate. The ground covered during the course provides the economic foundations for the more specialist economic courses available in the second year.

For the second year, the following classes are offered, although not all will actually be taught in any one year:

(1)   Functional Specialisms

  (i)   Quantitative Methods
 (ii)   Uses of Social Data in Public Policy
(iii)   Organisational Behaviour and Analysis
 (iv)   Financial Planning and Management.

(2)   Area Specialisms

  (i)   Government and Industry
 (ii)   Public Finance
(iii)   Health Policy and Administration
 (iv)   Educational Policy and Administration
  (v)   Housing Policy and Administration
 (vi)   Social Services
(vii)   Leisure and Recreation
 (vi)   Public Utilities and Enterprise
(vii)   Urban Development and Politics
(viii) Transport Planning and Policy
 (ix)   Inter-governmental Relations.

The dissertation will be an original piece of work. It will normally be concerned with a particular policy and its problems or the application of particular approaches and techniques to the analysis of policy. It should be completed by the end of the academic year in which the curriculum is completed.

Author Index

References from Notes indicated by 'n' after page reference

Abel-Smith, B. 91n, 92n
Allison, G. 34, 38n, 39n
Altschuler, A. 66n
Anderson, R.W. 89n
Argyris, C. 10, 20, 21n

Baker, R.J.S. 72, 88n
Barker, A. 91n
Barry, B. 16, 18, 22n
Beckman, N. 37n
Bennington, J. 89n
Bennis, W. 10, 11, 12, 20n, 21n
Berger, P. 21n
Bish, R.L. 16, 22n
Brittan, S. 103n
Brostek, M. 65n, 67n
Brown, R.G.S. 72, 87n, 88n
Bullock, R.E.H. 89n
Burns, T. 39n, 71, 74, 75, 90n

Caiden, G.E. 37n
Campbell, A. 65n
Carroll, J.D. 65n, 67n
Castenada, C. 21n
Chadwick, G. 90n
Chapman, R.A. 64n, 78-9, 89, 87n,
   88n, 89n, 91n, 92n, 94, 102n,
   103n
Charlesworth, J.C. 19n, 88n
Charlton, J. 92n
Cherns, A.B. 38n
Child, J. 75, 90n
Chomsky, N. 37n
Civil Service Department, 103n
Cleland, D.I. 21n
Cockburn, C. 89n
Coleman, J.S. 37n
Committee on the Civil Service
   (Fulton) 89n
Coplin, W.D. 65n
Crecine, J.P. 53, 66n
Crozier, M. 39n, 75
Culyer, A.J. 89n
Cyert, R.M. 33, 39n

Dahl, R.A. 6, 37n
Dahrendorf, R. 103n
Davies, B. 90n
Dawson, R.E. 37n
Dearlove, J. 90n

Diesing, P. 33, 39n
Donnison, D. 89n
Downs, A. 16, 17, 22n
Dror, Y. 37n, 38n, 39n, 64n, 81,
   85, 93n
Dunn, W.L. 64n
Dunsire, A. 74-5, 88n, 90n, 91n
Dye, T.R. 23, 37n, 38n

Eddison, Tony 89n
Edwards, J. 92n
Egger, R. 37n
Ericson, R.F. 37n
Etzioni, A. 39n
Evan, W.M. 103n
Eversley, D. 89n

Faludi, A. 90n
Fesler, J.W. 20n
Ford Foundation, The 64n
Fox, A. 12, 21n
Friend, J.K. 89n, 90n
Fritschler, A.L. 41, 42, 62, 64n,
   65n
Fry, B.R. 90n
Fry, G.K. 87n

Garnett, J.L. 65n, 67n
Garrett, J. 89n
Gaus, J. 19n
Gawthrop, L.C. 39n
Glendinning, J.W., 89n
Golembiewski, R.T. 20n, 22n
Goodin, R.E. 22n
Gordon, I. 25, 98, 103n
Graymer, LeRoy 66n, 67n
Greenwood, R. 89n, 90n
Gunn, L.A. 65n

Hague, D.C. 91n
Hampden-Turner, C. 21n
Hart, D. 90n
Heclo, H. 66n, 89n, 103n
Henderson, K. 6, 19n, 20n, 21n
Henry, N. 20n
Hickson, D.J. 90n
Hill, M. 88n
Hinings, C.R. 89n, 90n, 91n
Hitch, C. 37n
Hofferbert, R.I. 37n

Honey, J.C. 102n
Hood, C.C. 88n, 90n
Horowitz, I.L. 37n

Jacob, H. 90n
Jenkins, W.I. 38n, 76, 88n, 91n, 92n
Jessop, W.N. 89n, 90n
Jones, C.O. 37n

Katz, J.E. 37n
Keeling, D. 8n
King, W.R. 21n
King Edwards Hospital Fund 92n
Kirkhart, L. 20n
Klein, R. 88n, 89n

Lambright, W.H. 22n
Lasswell, H. 23, 36n, 37n
Lawrence, P.R. 90n
Lerner, D. 23, 36n
Levy, F.J. 66n
Lewis, J. 25, 103n
Likert, R. 10, 12
Lindblom, C.I. 33, 39n
Lipsky, M. 90n
Lomer, M. 89n
Lorsch, J. 90n
Luckman, T. 21n
Lyden, F.J. 39n

McGregor, D. 10, 20n
McKean, R. 37n
Mackenzie, W.J.M. 20n, 91n
Mackleprang, A.J. 41, 42, 62, 64n, 65n
McLoughlin, B.J. 90n
Maass, A. 37n.
Mair, R. 103n
March, J.G. 20n, 33, 39n
Marini, F. 14, 20n, 21n, 22n
Maslow, A. 10, 12, 20n, 21n
Meltsner, A. 38n, 66n, 91n
Miller, E.G. 39n
Mills, C.Wright 12, 21n
Molitor, A. 70, 87n
Mosher, F.C. 5n, 20n, 21n, 37n, 39n
Moynihan, D.P. 28, 29, 30, 38n, 57, 95, 103n
Myers, C.S. 87n

NASPAA (National Association of Schools of Public Affairs and Administration) 5n, 9, 40-42, 47-8, 51, 59, 60, 63, 64, 65n,

101, 102
NIIP (National Institute of Industrial Psychology)70
New Local Authorities: management and structure 89n
Newton, K. 88n
Newton, T. 89n
Niskanen, W. 16, 17, 22n
Novick, D. 39n

Ostrom, V. 6, 16, 17, 20n, 22n

Parris, H. 87n
Peacock, A.T. 89n, 92n
Pendleton, W.C. 67n
Perrow, C. 12, 21n
Peters, G.H. 89n
Pettigrew, A.M. 39n
Pirsig, R.M. 21n
Plowden, W. 103n
Power, J.M. 90n
Public Administration 80
Public Administration Bulletin 80, 91n
Public Administration Review 43
Pugh, D.S. 75, 90n

Quade, E.S. 23, 28, 37n

Rackoff, S. 90n
Ranson, S. 89n, 90n
Reich, C. 21n
Rhodes, R.A.W. 37n, 65n, 88n, 92n, 103n
Ridley, F.F. 69, 70, 87n, 88n, 91n, 92n, 103n
Rivlin, A. 30, 38n, 57
Roberts, G.K. 92n
Robinson, J.A. 37n
Robson, W.A. 70,71, 87n, 88n, 91n, 92n
Rose, M. 21n, 70, 87n
Rose, R. 88n, 92n, 103n
Rourke, R.E. 66n

Salaman, G. 91n
Schaefer, G. 90n
Schick, A. 6, 20n, 61, 66n
Seidman, H. 66n
Self, P. 18, 22n, 88n, 89n
Sharpe, L.J. 38n, 88n, 94, 96, 100, 102, 103n
Silverman, D. 21n
Simeon, R. 39n
Simon, H.A. 6, 16, 32, 33, 38n, 39n

Sinclair, R. 38n
Skitt, J. 89n
Slater, P.E. 21n
Smith, B.C. 88n
Smith, B.L.R. 37n, 50n
Smith, D.G. 5n
Spiers, M. 89n
Stalker, G.M. 74, 75, 90n
Stanford University 66n
Stanyer, J. 88n, 91n
Starforth, M. 92n
Steel, D. 91n, 92n
Stewart, J.D. 87n., 88n, 89n
Stone, A.B. 5n, 65n
Stone, D.C. 5n, 65n

Thomas, R.M. 69, 70, 87n
Thompson, J.D. 91n
Thompson, K. 91n
Thompson, S. 90n
Thompson, V. 15, 21n
Tiebout, C.M. 17, 22n
Times Higher Educational
    Supplement 1, 88n
Titmuss, R.M. 91n, 92n
Toffler, A. 11, 21n
Townsend, P. 91n
Tullock, G. 16, 22n

Van Gunsteren, H.R. 39n
Vickers, Sir Geoffrey 76-7, 91n

Waldo, D. 5n, 6, 9, 14, 15, 20n,
    22n, 23, 36, 37n, 39n, 69, 87n
Walker, J. 38n, 53, 54, 66n
Wamsley, G. 22n
Warren, R. 22n
Weinberg, R.M. 66n
Weiner, H. 38n
Weiss, C. 38n
White, M.J. 39n
White, O.F. 20n
Wildavsky, A. 2, 23, 28, 37n, 39n,
    52, 57, 66n, 89n, 103n
Wilensky, H. 38n
Williams, A. 89n, 92n
Williams, O.P. 18, 22n
Winters, R. 90n
Wiseman, J. 89n, 92n
Wolin, S. 13, 15, 21n
Woodward, J. 71, 74, 75, 90n
Wright, D.S. 103

Yates, D.T. 43, 52, 64n, 66n
Yewlett, C.J.L. 90n
Young, K. 25, 90n, 103n

Zald, M. 22n
Zimring, B. 21n

118

Subject Index

Analytical techniques 26, 27, 28, 42, 43, 62, 63, 65n, 100-101
    distinction between consumers/technicians 52-3, 54, 55, 57, 63
    in UK masters' degrees 79, 85, 100-101

'British Brookings' 1, 72, 97-8, 103n
Brookings Institution, the 26, 103n
Budgeting 15, 42, 43, 50
Business schools: in UK 80, 92n
                  in USA 2, 9, 58, 59, 66n

Centre for Studies in Social Policy 79, 103n
Civil Service College 79, 95, 103n
Contextual Courses 52-3, 54, 55, 57, 63
Corporate planning 73, 83
Cost Benefit Analysis 26, 43, 73
Critical Path Analysis 73
Curriculum design 3, 42, 44-5, 45-7, 51-2, 55, 57, 62-3, 83-4,
    110-111; and organisational form 45, 49-50, 53, 57, 61-2, 85-6

Decision-making models: rational model 29, 30-31, 32, 63
                        organisational model 30, 32-3, 62, 66n, 75, 101
                        political model 30-31, 33-4, 63

Evaluation 24, 25, 26, 29, 30
Experiential teaching methods 43, 51-2, 56, 63, 84-5, 100-101, 102

Fabians, the 26, 69, 70
Focused masters' programmes 40, 49, 50, 57-8, 59, 60-61, 63, 101-2
Ford Foundation, the 5n, 42-3, 52, 67n, 85, 99

Graduate School of Business (Stanford) 1-2, 40, 43, 58-59, 108-11
    curriculum 58
    faculty specialisms 59
    focused approach 59, 60
Graduate School of Public Policy (Berkeley) 1-2, 40, 42, 55-58, 62-3,
    84, 107-8
    curriculum 55
    faculty specialisms 55
    focused approach 57, 60
    organisational characteristics 57

Inclusive masters' programmes 40, 47, 48, 49, 50, 51, 54, 60, 63, 65n,
    101, 101-2
Industrial Administration Research Unit 71, 90n
Information for policy 24, 25, 26
Institute of Local Government Studies (Birmingham) 2, 68, 78, 79, 80-86,
    93n, 98, 111-2
    curriculum 83-4, 111-2
    faculty specialisms 83
    organisational characteristics 81, 82, 85-6

Institute of Public Policy Studies (Michigan) 1-2, 40, 43, <u>51-54</u>, 106-7
  curriculum 51-2, 106-7
  faculty specialisms 52
  inclusive approach 54, 60
  organisational characteristics 53-4
Institute of Social and Economic Research 80, 89n
Intergovernmental relations 19, 103n

Legal-institutional studies 62, 64n, 70-71
Locational choice 17-8, 22n
London School of Economics and Political Science 80, 91n, 92n, 103n

Management 8, 26, 50, 82
Management by objectives 73
Masters' degrees
  in UK 78-80
    Institute of Local Government Studies (Birmingham) 80-86, 111-2
    School for Advanced Urban Studies (Bristol), 113-4
    University of Strathclyde 114-5
    <u>See also</u> entries for each institution
  in USA 1-2, 40-43
    Graduate School of Public Policy (Berkeley) 55-8, 107-8
    Graduate School of Business (Stanford) 58-9, 108-11
    Institute of Public Policy Studies (Michigan) 51-4, 106-7
    Maxwell School (Syracuse) 43-51, 104-6
    <u>See also</u> entries for each institution
Maxwell School (Syracuse) 1-2, 40, <u>43-51</u>, 104-6
  curriculum 44-5, 45-7, 104-6
  faculty specialisms 45
  inclusive approach 47-9, 50-51, 60
  organisational characteristics 45, 49-50
Micro-economics, <u>See</u> Political economy

NASPAA (National Association of Schools of Public Affairs and
  Administration)9, 40-43, 45, 47-9, 50, 59, 63, 65n, 98, 101, 102
NIESR (National Institute for Economic and Social Research)74, 79
NIIP (National Institute of Industrial Psychology)70
National Health Service 80,90n
'New' Public Administration 14-5, 19, 21n

Organisational humanism 9, 10-13, 14, 20n, 21n
Organisational sociology 72, 74, 74-6, 100
Organisation theory 8, 18-9, 20n, 42, 58, 59, 62-3, 66n, 72, 76, 79,
  83, 101

PEP (Political and Economic Planning) 74, 79, 90n, 103n
PPBS (Planning-programming-budgeting-systems) 26, 30 35, 57, 73
Personnel management 11, 26, 42, 43, 50
Planning 74, 90n
Policy advocacy 24, 25, 26
Policy analysis
  and clients 27, 56
  definition 24, 27-8
  and dichotomy between prescription/description 29, 30, 35, 38n, 101
  disciplinary basis 27, 28, 36, 60
  origins 9, 26-7

and prediction 28, 35, 77
and Public Administration 1, 19, 28, 36, 38n, 42-3, 61, 101
and roles of social scientists 28-30, 35, 61
teaching 42-3; (See also Graduate School of Public Policy, Graduate
            School of Business, Institute of Public Policy
            Studies, Maxwell School)
and theories of decision-making 30-35
in UK 72-3; (See also Institute of Local Government Studies, School
            for Advanced Urban Studies, University of Strathclyde)
Policy analysts, employment of 38n, 59, 63, 67n, 97, 99
Policy content 24, 25, 26
Policy outputs 24, 25, 26, 73, 73-4
Policy studies 24, 25, 26
Political economy 9, 16-8, 19, 22n
Political theory 9, 13-5, 19
Polytechnics, See Undergraduate teaching
Public Administration
   definition 5n, 7-9
   disciplinary basis 6-7, 8-9, 14, 36, 41, 60, 71, 97, 101
   and political science 6, 8, 9, 40-41, 68, 73, 95
   in UK 68-78
      American influence on 72-4, 77-8, 82, 86; (See also Organisational
                        sociology, social critic, QNGs)
      future development 98-9, 102, 103n
      teaching 78-80, 92n. 113-15; (See also Institute of Local Govern-
         ment Studies, School for Advanced Urban Studies, Undergraduate
         teaching, University of Strathclyde)
      tradition 69-71, 76-8
   in USA 6-22
      current developments 10-18; (See also Organisational humanism,
         Policy analysis, Political economy, Political theory)
      origins 6
      teaching 40-43, 78-80; (See also Masters' degrees, Curriculum
                                    design)
   USA and UK compared 68-9, 94-7
   variety of approaches 7, 9, 18-9, 35, 36, 40, 57, 78, 97, 98, 99,
      101, 102
Public Administration Committee 80, 98
Public Policy-making
   variety of approaches 23-7
   and policy analysis 27-8

QNGs 72, 77-8, 91n

Rand Corporation, the 26, 37n, 43
Relevance 26-7, 36
Resources 4, 26, 36, 42-3, 68, 71, 73, 86, 86-7, 94, 95, 98-9
Royal Institute of Public Administration 80, 98

SSRC (Social Science Research Council) 72, 86, 97, 98, 99
School for Advanced Urban Studies (Bristol) 79, 96, 113-4
Self-actualising 12, 13
Social critic 70, 76-7
Social scientists,
   roles of 28-30, 35, 61
   in UK 94-6

Stanford University, See Graduate School of Business (Stanford)
'Sublimation of politics' 13
Syracuse University, See Maxwell School (Syracuse)

Undergraduate teaching
   in Polytechnics 78, 79, 92n
   in UK 78, 79, 92n
   in USA 5n
University of Aston, See Industrial Administration Research Unit
University of Birmingham, See Institute of Local Government Studies
University of Bristol, See School for Advanced Urban Studies
University of California (Berkeley), See Graduate School of Public
                                        Policy
University of Michigan, See Institute of Public Policy Studies
University of Strathclyde 78, 114-15
Urban Studies 9, 16, 19, 67n

Watergate 9, 13, 21n; See also entries under Relevance